Edward I's Granddaughters

Edward I's Granddaughters

Murder, Power and Plantagenets

Louise Wyatt

PEN & SWORD HISTORY

First published in Great Britain in 2023 by
Pen & Sword History
An imprint of Pen & Sword Books Limited
Yorkshire – Philadelphia

Copyright © Louise Wyatt 2023

ISBN 978 1 39900 670 5

Typeset by Mac Style
Printed in the UK by CPI Group (UK) Ltd, Croydon, CR0 4YY.

Pen & Sword Books Limited incorporates the imprints of After
the Battle, Atlas, Archaeology, Aviation, Discovery, Family History,
Fiction, History, Maritime, Military, Military Classics, Politics,
Select, Transport, True Crime, Air World, Frontline Publishing, Leo
Cooper, Remember When, Seaforth Publishing, The Praetorian Press,
Wharncliffe Local History, Wharncliffe Transport, Wharncliffe True
Crime and White Owl.

For a complete list of Pen & Sword titles please contact

PEN & SWORD BOOKS LIMITED
47 Church Street, Barnsley, South Yorkshire, S70 2AS, England
E-mail: enquiries@pen-and-sword.co.uk
Website: www.pen-and-sword.co.uk
or
PEN AND SWORD BOOKS
1950 Lawrence Rd, Havertown, PA 19083, USA
E-mail: Uspen-and-sword@casematepublishers.com
Website: www.penandswordbooks.com

In loving memory of my triumvirate of strong women that I didn't appreciate enough at the time. My mum, my nan and Pat, my ever-patient mother-in-law. Love you, miss you.

Contents

Acknowledgements

As well as the array of friendly and supportive historical writing groups on social media, I would like to give especial thanks to the genealogist Brad Verity of Palm Springs, California, for the amount of information he sent me after my initial enquiries regarding his paper 'Love Matches and Contracted Misery: Thomas of Brotherton and his Daughters (Part 1)'. Not only did he share much of his own research with me, he signposted me to references and sources I would never have found by myself. His work is meticulous and a highly recommended read, available at https://fmg.ac. I'd also like to thank the historian and author Kathryn Warner for allowing me to use her translation regarding Alice of Norfolk's attack and for having such a wonderful blog where you will find a wealth of information to do with the players of the fourteenth century right here at www.edwardthesecond.blogspot. Her research is meticulous and followed up with primary and secondary sources that helped me enormously when following links for my own research. Also many thanks to Claire Noble of Core History for tracing the original fourteenth century document and specific membrane quoted in the Complete Peerage that recorded Alice's fate.

Introduction

I discovered Alice of Norfolk whilst falling down the proverbial research rabbit hole for another book concerning Chepstow in Monmouthshire and past custodians of the earldom, the lands and the castle. It was her father I discovered first, Thomas of Brotherton, Earl of Norfolk from 1312 until his death in 1338, and yet I had never heard of him. Researching him was an eye-opener; the firstborn son of the mighty Edward I and his second wife, Marguerite of France, and therefore a younger half-brother to Edward II, a vast landowner and member of the ruling wealthy elite as well as a Plantagenet, why wasn't this man better known? Thomas appears to have failed to make any mark on history, unlike his contemporary peers such as the earl of Salisbury.

Whilst researching Thomas, I came upon his unconventional marriage, and his historically famous daughter, but it was his younger daughter, Alice, and her tragic story that jumped off the pages at me. The need to put her story out there was overwhelming. Alice was born into the ruling powerhouse of the Plantagenets, her uncle would be the future Edward II, and her first cousin, the future Edward III. No known description of Alice exists; unfortunately, not much exists about her at all. There are sources that describe her paternal grandmother, Queen Marguerite, and her mother, Alice Hales, as beautiful, as well as her much more famous first cousin Joan of Kent, so it is within the realms of possibility that Alice of Norfolk was of an attractive countenance. Despite being the daughter of a king's brother, albeit half-brother, the lack of information regarding Alice Plantagenet of Norfolk is acutely disappointing. Born into prestige and wealth, she joined a brother, Edward, the heir to the earldom of Norfolk, and an older sister, Margaret, who went on to be a very powerful noblewoman and the Duchess of Norfolk in her own right.

It is essential to give some context to the times Alice was living in: the high mortality rates; the first wave of the plague that hit Alice's home territory of East Anglia the hardest; the social demands on someone of Alice's standing; early marriages and the dangers (as well as high rates) of childbearing; all these affected Alice of Norfolk in one way or another.

The fourteenth century wasn't a particularly good one for England. Political instability, civil war, decimation of the ruling elite (seven earls being executed by 1330) and setting a precedent for the deposition of an anointed king.[1] Global socio-economic disasters engulfed rich and poor alike, including floods, droughts, plague and famine. The Great Flood and subsequent Great Famine of 1315–1322 saw excessive rainfall throughout 1315, 1316 and 1317 result in poor harvests and starvation, especially for the lower echelons of society, leading to reports of cannibalism and a sharp increase in crime.[2] Indeed, Norfolk (along with Essex and Yorkshire) saw a 200 per cent increase in crime during 1315–1319 compared to the average of the preceding years (1300–1314). This was mainly theft of clothing and food, indicating destitution and desperation.[3] In 1319, due to a non-volcanic but natural 'transitory global environmental event between 1300 and 1353', around the time of Easter, there was a cattle plague in England, spreading over the following months and resulting in an estimated sixty-two per cent death rate of the bovine population.[4] This led to a severe decline in dairy production, manure and oxen for haulage and ploughing, making agricultural recovery after the famine increasingly difficult. Meat production, which depended on salt for long term storage, was decimated by the failure of salt production due to 'inundating rains'. In the Middle Ages, only enough meat to cover two harvests at the most could be stored.[5] The famine-induced widespread collapse of agriculture often led to debt, forced land sales, and poverty. However, by the spring of 1349 a new and terrifying disease called the plague – which had arrived in Dorset in 1348 – hit East Anglia with devastating effect.[6]

The plague spread, mainly through trade routes, up into Sudbury, Suffolk, in early March 1349. By the end of April it had spread throughout East Anglia and by March 1350 is estimated to have killed over half the region's population[7]. William Bateman, Bishop of Norwich from 1344 to 1355, lost two-thirds of his diocese to the disease (the diocese in the fourteenth century covered Norfolk, Suffolk and parts of Cambridge).[8] Although not every death can be attributed to the plague, the institution of new priests varied from nine to nineteen per month from January to April 1349, accelerating to seventy-three new incumbents in May, 120 in June, 222 in July and 145 in August, before dropping off after September, showing just how virulent the plague was during the summer months.[9] The bishop went on to establish Trinity Hall, Cambridge, in 1350, specifically to train new priests following the decimation of the clergy.

The plague would strike again in 1361, 1369 and 1375, leading to societal changes amongst the peasants and nobility (e.g., the peasants' revolt in 1381). And it would have horrific consequences for Alice's family and her lineage. Her two eldest children, including Edward, the one son and heir, are not mentioned again after July 1349, and it would be easy to surmise that they were lost in the first and most devastating plague outbreak of the same year. However, child mortality was high regardless of the plague and children were fifteen to twenty times more likely to die from conditions such as tuberculosis and any numerous childhood diseases such as measles, with both children and adults four to eight times as likely to die from any number of infections than the plague[10]. It is also worth remembering that childbirth was the cause of death for many medieval women, high or low born. However, a recent study has found that medieval childbirth wasn't necessarily as dangerous as previously thought. It was dangerous in the sense of hygiene and the lack of knowledge regarding infections and prophylactic ways to combat disease, but it can be considered that a high rate of pregnancies with a short interim between births, as well as maternal age and multiple births, would cause approximately one in twenty deaths related to childbirth[11].

It is worth keeping these facts in mind when the narrative repeats the assumed cause of death through plague and childbirth.

In March 1324, against the backdrop of all this socio-economic mayhem, a future king of Scotland was born in Dunfermline Abbey. The future David II of Scotland, son of Robert Bruce, aged four, was betrothed to the seven-year-old Joan of the Tower, youngest daughter of Edward II and Alice of Norfolk's cousin, in July 1328. Around the same time, a female child, Alice of Norfolk, was born into wealth and privilege. She was the second daughter to the 1st Earl of Norfolk, Thomas of Brotherton, and his first wife. It is highly possible that Alice of Norfolk was born at Bungay Castle or the nearby manor of Earl Soham, although the family seat was Framlingham Castle, birthplace of Alice's older sister, Margaret of Norfolk, c.1322. Records indicate that Thomas wasn't at Framlingham around the time of Alice's birth. In the dead stock accounts of 1324–25, Framlingham was unusually sparsely furnished and in the 1327 subsidy returns (taxation), Thomas of Brotherton owed 7s for Earl Soham but nothing for Framlingham Castle. Bungay Castle would also have been fit for a prince as it had been extensively refortified a few years previously, c.1294, by Roger Bigod, the previous Earl of Norfolk, and remained a well-maintained castle at this time.[12]

Alice of Norfolk's exact date of birth is unknown, though we can narrow it down to possibly the first quarter of 1324. We know Alice was married at her father's death in August 1338 so must have been aged at least fourteen, the legal age for a girl to marry. In terms of inheritance, boys and girls had to be twenty-one to inherit from the Crown (tenant-in-chief), although girls could inherit at around fifteen years old if they were married[13]. At Easter 1344, Alice is noted as being underage when dealing with a writ concerning a tenant but appears to have come of age a year later (therefore aged twenty-one) as her father's co-heir in March 1345 when her husband, Edward Montagu, was pardoned £50 of the relief (a form of inheritance tax) due from Alice as one of the co-heirs and daughters of the late Earl of Norfolk. This would put Alice of Norfolk's date of birth as around March[14].

There is not enough history about Alice of Norfolk for a book solely on her life. This book, therefore, also explores her more famous sister, her father the earl, and certain members of her larger Plantagenet family whilst maintaining direct links to the Norfolk Plantagenets. I have tried to keep the narrative linked to Alice, or at least her father, throughout all chapters and there is a special connection with her in the chapter on her cousin, Edward III. Alice lived in tumultuous times and was related to well-known historical people so there was a good amount of material to examine those around her. I hope this book goes some way to giving Alice of Norfolk, the forgotten Plantagenet noblewoman, a voice.

There are many variations in the name and titles of what Alice and her family were known by over the years. For consistency and definition with the main subjects of this book, as well as avoiding long-winded repetitiveness, I have stuck with using their basic names as opposed to titles: Thomas of Brotherton, (his wife) Alice Hales, and their offspring, Edward of Norfolk, Margaret of Norfolk and Alice of Norfolk, as well as Thomas' brother Edmund of Woodstock, the doomed Earl of Kent. I have referred to the son and heir of Edward III, Edward of Woodstock, as the 'Black Prince' (although that nickname was used after his death, I have used it here to distinguish him from other Edwards).

I have tried to avoid vague words such as 'supposed' and 'assumed' but unfortunately, due to the dearth of information and history regarding Alice, sometimes the generics cannot be avoided. The conclusions are my own and there may be more academic reasonings out there but, at the end of the day, Alice's existence is barely recorded. No one knows why she was so brutally attacked by her husband, and unless something comes to light post-publication of this book, it will more than likely stay a mystery.

Chapter 1

The Murdered Granddaughter –
Alice of Norfolk

Expectancy as a Noblewoman of the Fourteenth Century

In the fourteenth century female children of elite households didn't necessarily have an easy life; they would be taught from a young age how to budget, run an estate, the art of delegation, organisation of feasts, sewing/embroidery, appropriate behaviour and the administration of a large household, as would be expected of them when they married.[1] Daughters, although they could be sent away to be educated at a convent or another noble house, tended to be taught at home, acquiring social and practical skills befitting of their social standing. Indeed, the paternal aunt of Alice, the nun-princess Mary of Woodstock, often had tutelage over her many nieces, and, on occasion, her half-brothers Thomas of Brotherton and Edmund of Woodstock when they were young. After the age of twelve daughters were then considered adolescents and were usually married by fourteen, with their dowries and financial arrangements between bride and groom having been arranged at a very young age.[2]

As we have seen, economic uncertainty was rife in the fourteenth century and life expectancy was extremely short; many people died before their thirtieth birthday. As the age of twenty-one was the age one could inherit their lands direct from the Crown, it is easy to see why daughters were treated as adults at a much earlier age than we would consider appropriate and why they could be expected to bear children in their teens.[3] It was quite the norm for the noble daughter to have children by her mid-twenties; women were considered in their prime by their late teenage years, mature by twenty-five and – assuming they survived disease and childbirth – getting on a bit by their thirties.[4] The second daughter of Thomas of Brotherton, Earl of Norfolk, Alice of Norfolk, had borne five children by the time of her death shortly before her twenty-eighth birthday.

However, this wasn't necessarily the way for all medieval noblewomen. Eleanora, eldest surviving daughter of Edward I and another aunt of Alice of Norfolk, for example, whilst betrothed young did not marry until her early twenties. It must be remembered that medieval noble and royal marriage arrangements were born out of political machinations, not usually romance (although that did happen on occasion), hence the arrangements to seal mighty alliances as soon as was possible in childhood. *The Mirrors of Princes*, a series of medieval treatises that advised and guided world rulers of the principles of knightly conduct and legalities, was utilised by the Italian scholar, theologian and advisor, Thomas Aquinas (1225–1274) and appears to have been heeded by the nobility during this period. Aquinas advised that women should not procreate before the age of eighteen and men to refrain from sexual conduct until they reached twenty-one. However, in her 1997 thesis on the *Medieval Maiden*, Phillips notes that, 'The ages from seven to twenty-one represent a cloudy, ill-defined period in the life cycle of both girls and boys according to different forms of law.' There are a few examples of nobility bearing very early births, one being the future Margaret Beaufort, mother of Henry VII, who nearly died giving birth to him aged thirteen.[5] In fact, Alice of Norfolk had her first two children between the age of fourteen – when we know she was married – and nineteen – when her son and daughter had their marriage betrothals arranged. Over the next six years she had three more children, her last born in February 1349.

However, noblewomen were not necessarily the pliant, conforming ideal of medieval womanhood that history would perhaps have us believe. They had time to pursue their passions and could be rather formidable, as in the case of Alice's sister, Margaret of Norfolk, who will be discussed in the next chapter.

It was, however, a fine line – wield too much independence and one could be accused of witchcraft, as in the case of Joan of Navarre

(1368–1437). Joan was the second wife of Alice's distant cousin, the future king Henry IV. Originally viewed with suspicion by the English, Joan maintained good relations with her stepchildren, one of whom would become king Henry V, and proved instrumental in various political truces[6]. A rather rich widow in 1419 (an annual income of approximately £4 million in today's value), Joan was accused of using sorcery and witchcraft to hasten the death of her stepson, Henry V. Their relationship had always been positive, and Henry had treated her well after the death of his father, her husband, but the success of battles such as Agincourt drained the coffers and Henry coveted Joan's wealth. By accusing her of witchcraft – although the accusation wasn't from him directly – but not putting her on trial, Henry could astutely confiscate her wealth.[7]

This fine line was trodden more successfully by Alice's cousin by marriage, Philippa of Hainault (c.1313/14–1369), wife of Edward III, first cousin to Alice. Although the usual marriage of political machinations, it turned out to be a very successful and companionable partnership. Philippa is known to have accompanied Edward III on his incursions and his early campaigns of the Hundred Years War, for example. She often acted as intercessor for acts of mercy for ordinary people, including the incident where Philippa intervened for clemency for negligent carpenters when a wooden stand that her and her ladies were standing on, at a tournament in Cheapside in 1331, collapsed.[8]

Another way a noblewoman had relative freedom from the domain of masculinity was entering into the convent way of life. An aunt of Alice, the royal nun-princess Mary of Woodstock (1278–c.1332), half-sister to Alice's father, Thomas of Brotherton, did just that and led an unusually free and well-travelled life. Mary was the fourth surviving daughter of Edward I and Eleanor of Castille, elder sister to Edward II, and entered Amesbury Priory in Wiltshire from 1285. But her life as a nun included access to rich clothing, travelling to her domains to see family, and gambling; hardly the vision of poverty, chastity and obedience one would expect from the Benedictine Rule.[9]

Alice shared the bloodline of women who were far from meek and pliant, but, unfortunately, very little is known about any interactions she may or may not have had with her relatives. She is mentioned in various documents throughout her life, but these are mainly due to events that incorporated her father, her husband, Edward Montagu, and her sister, Margaret of Norfolk, of whom there is far more written about, which will be explored in a later chapter.

Alice

Like many minor characters on the medieval stage, nothing appears to be known of Alice's childhood and her marriage arrangement was no different for someone of her social standing; in fact, she was part of a land deal. It was all about the politics, her dowry, the union of powerful families and landed estates, as well as her assumed ability to produce heirs.[10] On 3 February 1333, when Alice was around nine years old, her marriage alliance to William, the son and heir of Sir William Montagu (who would become the earl of Salisbury a few years later), close ally and friend to Edward III, was negotiated between him and her father. This betrothal between a nine-year-old girl and four-year-old boy was not only part of a powerful land transaction between Norfolk and Salisbury, but also a sign of Montagu's continued favour with his close friend Edward III by marrying into the royal family, as well as Brotherton playing the political game and keeping in with Edward's new men. This will be discussed later[11]. However, we know this marriage didn't happen as at the time of Thomas of Brotherton's death, sometime before 25 August 1338, Margaret and her sister Alice are officially named as co-heirs, with Alice's husband noted as Edward Montagu, Sir William Montagu's younger brother, and therefore uncle of her original betrothed:

Thomas earl Marshal.
    London. Inq. taken before Henry Darci, mayor of London and the Mug's escheator there, on Tuesday before the Decollation of St. John the Baptist, 12 Edward III. Parish of St. Mary Somersete. A

ruinous messuage with a void plot of land, wherein no one dares to dwell, nine shops, and eight solars, from whence there are paid to the abbot of Messyngdene 8s. quit rent yearly, held of the king in chief, as the whole city is. Margaret the wife of John de Segrave and Alice the wife of Edward de Monte Acuto are his next heirs.[12]

Why did Alice marry Edward Montagu and not his nephew, William, as originally planned? In her 1985 thesis study of the earls of Salisbury, Huntingdon, Suffolk and Northampton, Jennifer Parker suggests that Edward Montagu 'ran off with Alice and married her himself'[13] sometime between March 1337 (when Edward Montagu was knighted, along with his brother, Sir William, now the 1st Earl of Salisbury) and when we know they were married by, i.e., August 1338. Parker names John Montagu, younger son of Sir William Montagu and brother to William Junior, as Alice's original betrothed. In a 2006 study of Thomas of Brotherton, Marshall also states Alice's childhood betrothal in 1333 to John Montagu, not William Junior, and that Alice married Edward instead due to John's early death. However, John Montagu (c.1330–c.1390), younger brother to the proposed William, was betrothed and married to Margaret *suo jure* Baroness Monthermer, granddaughter of Joan of Acre, Alice's aunt, and did not die young. Sir William and Edward Montagu did have another brother, also called John, original son and heir, but he predeceased their father in 1317.

Indeed, the reason Alice wed the older Edward Montagu and not his nephew, William, the future 2nd Earl of Salisbury – who went onto to an unsuccessful marriage and eventual annulment with Alice's first cousin Joan of Kent, mother of the future Richard II – will more than likely remain unknown and one can only assume a fraction of conjecture, such as the death of her brother and therefore herself and her sister, Margaret, becoming wealthy heiresses. We know Alice must have married Edward Montagu between March 1337, when he was knighted, and August 1338, on the death of her father, making Alice around fourteen years old. Edward was approximately eight to ten years older than Alice, as we will see in a later chapter, and her original betrothed, William Montagu, was nine to ten years old. Was Edward knighted in 1337 due to his brother's close friendship with Edward III, as sometimes quoted? Was it also to make him a better marriage prospect for marrying into the royal family? After all, William, Alice's original betrothed, was the son and heir of an earl. Edward Montagu at this point could be seen as a penniless and landless younger brother of a great family, a mere squire in his elder brother's retinue in 1330.[14] Alice's aunt, Joan of Acre, had done just that with Ralph Monthermer when she married for the second time in secret – and far below her standing as a royal princess – and asked her father, Edward I, to knight her most loyal household servant, possibly hoping it would make the fact she was marrying him as a knight and not just a retainer easier to break the news to her family. It didn't, but Joan of Acre will be discussed later.

A protracted betrothal was expected of transactions such as this, given the ages of Alice and William in 1333 – nine and five years old respectively – and in this case, a betrothal of fifteen years to which Sir William Montagu held 'for the term of William's life or if he should die within fifteen years ... reversion to William, son of William de Montacute and Alice, daughter of Thomas and to the heirs of their bodies.'[15] Maybe, as she blossomed and Edward became of marriageable age, they were attracted to each other? Did Thomas know he was dying at this point and acquiesced in Alice marrying the older Montagu? At four years the elder, was Alice considered too old for William Junior, bearing in mind how much younger people could die in the medieval era? Nothing is noted in the records of either a reaction by Sir William or Edward III, or anybody for that matter.

Although the Montagu family will be studied in a later chapter, what do we know about Edward Montagu? He was the fourth but third surviving and youngest son of Sir William Montagu, 2nd Lord Montagu (c.1285–1319) and his wife, Elizabeth de Montfort (d.1354),[16] younger brother to William, the 1st Earl of Salisbury, who was a close friend and confidante of Edward III, and uncle to William, the future 2nd Earl of Salisbury. There is no recorded birth date of Edward, but he would have been quite a bit older than Alice, possibly by at least eight to ten years.[17] As a landless younger brother, he owed his good fortune to his brother William's close connections with Edward III, although William's generosity doesn't appear to extend to Edward as much as it did to their brother, Simon Montagu, Bishop of Worcester and Ely. Edward was a squire in Montagu's household in 1330,[18] which gives credence to the statement by the antiquarian George Wrottesley, writing in 1898, that Edward was present at the Nottingham Coup of 1330 that led to the arrest of Roger Mortimer, resulting in Edward III becoming king outright.[19] However, Wrottesley also notes, wrongly, that after he died in 1361 Edward Montagu left one only daughter, who married William Ufford, the Earl of 'Pembroke'. In actual fact, Edward Montagu left three daughters by Alice of Norfolk: Elizabeth, who had married Walter Ufford but died shortly after her father; Maud, who became a nun; and Joan, who did marry Walter's brother, William Ufford, who was the Earl of Suffolk, not Pembroke. By his second wife, Joan, about whom not a lot else is known, Edward also left a baby son, Edward, who followed his father to the grave shortly after, and another daughter, called Audrey.

By marrying Alice of Norfolk, a wealthy heiress and cousin to the king (let's not forget that she was the granddaughter of Edward I and also the great-granddaughter of King Phillip III of France through her paternal grandmother, Queen Marguerite), Edward acquired wealth and a social ladder to climb that he surely must have only ever dreamed about. His noted loutish behaviour and fierce reputation would prove true in future documented incidences and lead to their marriage ending in tragedy for Alice in 1352.[20]

Alice and Edward's marriage was nothing if not fruitful, and from what we do know their marriage appears to get off to a good start. Edward's military career appears steady, with some sources remarking it was a tad underwhelming and others noting he was a professional soldier. He had been awarded a grant to support his knighthood in March 1337[21] and was with the king in Antwerp in September 1338 where, along with others, his possessions and servants were given the king's protection whilst overseas[22]. In 1346 Edward served in the king's retinue and was engaged to swell the numbers of Edward III's household knights for the famous battle of Crécy heading up a total retinue of forty-four men, including nine knights, twenty archers and fifteen esquires. Thanks to the antiquarian, biographer and English army officer George Wrottesley (1827–1909), who used 'writs of exoneration' in the memoranda rolls of Walter de Wetewang, Treasurer of the King's Household between April 1344 and November 1347, we know some of the names in Edward's retinue. Sir William Carbonel, a knight of Suffolk, William Giffard, who had been a loyal member of Thomas of Brotherton's affinity[23], William Jermie [Jermy], whose family had married into Brotherton's family by marriage – Thomas' first wife and Alice's mother, Alice Hales, had a sister who married a Jermy – Henry Bacon, Walter de Walcote, Geoffrey Moubray (Mowbray family), John Goldynham of Bulmere, Robert Serle, who was Parson of St John of Ilketeshale (Ilketshall) from 1341 to 1351 and whose patron was the prioress of Bungay, John de Roos, Thomas Wayt and Hugh de Sandeby. Between 10 and 12 June 1355, Edward Montagu appointed attorneys and had letters of protection going abroad to Gascony in the retinue of his nephew, William, 2nd Earl of Salisbury, under the Black Prince in a rekindling of the Hundred Years War.[24]

Edward Montagu, therefore, fought in and survived some of the bloodiest, most violent battles of the fourteenth century. He was summoned to Parliament between 20 November 1348 to 1360, and had been made a peer in the form of lord of Bungay.[25] Bungay Castle appears to be the family seat and we know Alice was awarded the manor and borough of Bungay after Thomas of Brotherton's death in December 1338, and it was here their fifth and final child, Joan, was born in February 1349. By the end of 1349, however, things appear to go downhill very quickly.[26]

Alice's Children

Edward Montagu would have been a busy man when home from his military and royal service as Alice spent most of the 1340s having children. A son and daughter by the names of Edward and Audrey (also known as Etheldreda) were both born before 1343, though presumably at least one of them, if not both, had been born by 1340 as 'when the king was at Ghent in Flanders he took Edward's homage for all the lands which he and Alice held in chief of her inheritance, by reason of their common offspring.'[27] The king had been in Ghent from January 1340 where he had declared himself king of France[28]. By February 1349 Edward Junior and Audrey had been joined by three more sisters, namely Elizabeth, Maud and Joan respectively.

Edward and Audrey were most definitely born by March 1343 as their marriage contracts were arranged by their uncle, the Earl of Salisbury, to John and Blanche Mowbray, the children of John de Mowbray, 3rd Baron Mowbray, and his wife, Joan of Lancaster. The ceremony was arranged for 25 July that same year, but it was a double celebration that never occurred. Instead, John and Blanche Mowbray went on to marry the Montagu's first cousins, John and Elizabeth Segrave, children of Alice's sister, Margaret, and her first husband, Sir John Segrave, with negotiations beginning in March 1349[29]. It is interesting to note that Edward's brother, the Earl of Salisbury, was the one involved in the marriage arrangements of Edward's children, another sign that maybe he didn't trust his youngest brother's judgements in the same way he trusted their other surviving brother, the bishop, Simon.

Edward and Audrey Montagu were still alive and unmarried by July 1349, as the family, including the third child and second daughter, Elizabeth, were given permission by the Pope to choose their own confessors within the diocese of Norwich, a routine practice during the time of the plague. Edward and Alice's son, Edward, is noted as *donsel*, meaning 'a youth of high birth but not knighted'.[30] However, it appears that Edward and Audrey do not appear in records again and were most certainly dead by 1359, as was their mother. By this time, records show that the heirs of Alice were Elizabeth, aged fifteen and wife of Walter de Ufford, Maud, aged thirteen, and Joan, aged eleven, wife of William de Ufford.[31]

The plague had hit East Anglia hard in 1349 and it is reasonable to assume the two eldest children, one being Montagu's only son and heir, Edward Montagu, fell victim to this wave. Both children were last mentioned in July 1349, at the height of the plague, and we know it was ravaging Bungay at this time: 'the plague had broken out in the Benedictine Nunnery of Bungay and carried off the prioress amongst others'.[32] The plague victim prioress must have been Katarine/Katherine Falstaff, prioress since 1335.[33] The bishop of Norwich, William Bateman, on returning from France on the king's business, arrived via Yarmouth in May 1349 and made his way to Gillingham, Suffolk, the lands and property of his elder brother, Sir Bartholomew Bateman, who had also died by 7 June 1349[34]. From Gillingham on 13 June 1349, William Bateman instituted Lady Elene Ulesworth, a professed nun of Bungay, as the new prioress for Bungay, 'the bishop, of his special grace, provided the elect a woman sensible and discreet in both temporal and spiritual matters'.[35] She must have survived the plague as the next prioress of Bungay was a Lady Eleanor from 1360, and then in 1380 Katerina de Monte Acuto, Katherine Montagu, most likely the great-niece of Edward Montagu and discussed in the later chapter on the Montagu family[36].

Elizabeth Montagu (c.1344–September 1361) was the second eldest daughter and third child. Noted as married to Walter Ufford by 1359, aged fifteen years or more, Elizabeth died 'without heir of her body at Michaelmas, 35 Edward III'. This is a precise date of 29 September 1361, making her approximately seventeen years old at her death, although she may have died just before her father a month previously as her father's Inquisition Post Mortem, dated end of August 1361, states that the only remaining heir to Alice and Edward is their youngest daughter, Joan (Maud had entered a convent by the time of her father's death).[37]

Walter Ufford was more than likely an older brother of William Ufford but had predeceased his father[38]. Occasionally, Elizabeth is listed as being the daughter of Edward's second marriage to a lady called Joan, of unknown pedigree, and despite being married to Walter Ufford by age fifteen, it seems she was then contracted to marry again by January 1361. On 15 January 1361 at Bungay, a contract was drawn up for Sir John Braose (b.c.1339), son and heir of Sir Thomas Braose and Beatrice Mortimer, widow of Elizabeth's maternal uncle, Edward of Norfolk, to take 'Dame Elizabeth daughter of Sir Edward to wife'. The marriage should happen before the fortnight of 'St Hilary next' and included the manor of Tetbury, Gloucestershire, and some of the long-standing Braose lands. St Hilary is the religious day of 13 January, so presumably this meant they should marry within the year, as the agreement is dated 15 January. Or perhaps it means within the fortnight of the indenture. Elizabeth was still only sixteen, maybe seventeen at this point, and although Walter Ufford was still alive in 1351[39], he had predeceased his father, Earl Robert, who died in 1369. That's a bit of a time window, but Walter must have died at least by January 1361, and Elizabeth has to be the daughter of Alice and Edward, not his new wife, Joan, as sometimes mentioned in the antiquaries[40].

Sir John Braose was around twenty-two at the time of this indenture, a perfect age to wed Elizabeth, who, if she had been the daughter of her father's second wife, Joan, would be a mere babe-in-arms; that is, if there had been time to have a child between Edward and Joan's two-year-old daughter and three-month-old son at the time of Edward Montagu's death in July 1361. Edward Montagu's eldest child by Joan, as per his Inquisition Post Mortem, was the two-year-old Audrey, therefore born in the spring/summer of 1359, meaning he would have likely been married again by 1358. Another sign that Elizabeth is Alice's daughter is the statement in the indenture that 'Sir Thomas and Sir John grant that all matters and covenants spoken or treated of between the countess marshal and them in regard to the marriage shall be discharged.' This would have been Thomas of Brotherton's widow, Mary, Alice of Norfolk's stepmother as well as John Braose's aunt, who was known as Mary, Countess of Norfolk, Marshal of England, until she died a year later, so she would have had a keen interest in the arrangements.[41] Although ultimately, the marriage arrangements of Edward Montagu and Alice's children had been granted to him by the king after Alice's death in January 1352.

As we have seen, Elizabeth is not mentioned in her father's Inquisition Post Mortem, meaning she had most likely died, or was about to, at the time of his death and one can't help but consider yet again the effects of the second plague epidemic in the area at this time in 1361. Sir Thomas Braose also died in this year and his son, Sir John, had died by May 1367 with no male heirs from his marriage to Elizabeth, and thus reverted the lands of Tetbury to Beatrice, widow of Sir Thomas.[42]

The third daughter and fourth child Maud (c.1346–1393) entered Barking Abbey and took the veil on 16 November 1362, aged approximately sixteen, which means she must have been a novice nun for at least a couple of years previous to this. We have seen in the records that in 1359 her sisters, Elizabeth and Joan, were married to the Ufford brothers and Maud isn't married, despite being older than Joan, so was more than likely a nun at this point. With royal assent, Maud became the Abbess of Barking Abbey on 20 April 1377, following in the footsteps of her two aunts, Maud and Isabel, both sisters of her father, Edward Montagu. Her namesake, Maud Montagu, was abbess from 1341 to 1352, and Isabel Montagu from 1352 to 1358[43]. In 1362 the abbey was granted money for the life of Maud from the rent of her family's estates by licence from the father-in-law of her sisters, Elizabeth and Joan:

'1362. July 19. Licence for Robert de Ufford, earl of Suffolk, and Thomas his son, to Westminster, grant in mortmain to the abbess and convent of Berkyng, for the life of Maud de Mountagu, one of the nuns, 300 marks of rent out of the manor of Walsham, co. Suffolk, held in chief, and the manors of Baudeseye, Wykham, Hikelyngge and Chiselford, with power to distrain for the same if in arrear'.[44]

Maud outlived all her siblings, as well as her parents, and is noted as deceased in a writ dated 5 October 1393 for license for a new abbess at Barking Abbey[45].

Joan Montagu (1349–1375), the fifth and youngest child, was born at Bungay Castle, as noted previously. Joan was to be the sole heir of her mother's estates and would become the future countess of Suffolk. We have seen that Joan was married to William Ufford by 1359, aged approximately eleven, and William (c.1339–1382) was about ten years older than her. William became the 2nd Earl of Suffolk in 1369 on the death of his father, Robert, 1st Earl of Suffolk (b.1298) after the firstborn son and heir, also Robert, had died sometime before June 1368[46]. William likely had three older brothers, which would explain why his early years aren't recorded[47]. In 1878 a detailed genealogy was published by the antiquarian Robert Edmond Chester Waters, giving the Ufford brothers a birth order of Robert, Thomas, Walter, William and John, with only William and John – who became a priest – surviving their father. This would explain why seven years previous to William becoming Earl of Suffolk, his father and older brother, Thomas, then the Ufford heir and not William, were noted as granting money for life to Maud as detailed above, and why Alice of Norfolk's elder daughter, Elizabeth, and younger daughter, Joan, married Walter and William respectively.[48]

The Uffords had been linked to the royal household for generations and were from a local Suffolk landowning family, with William's great-grandfather, Robert (d.1298) being a younger son of John Peyton, changing his name to Ufford to represent his lordship via his good friendship with Edward I during the 1240s. During 1270–1274 he went on Crusade with Edward I, becoming his chief administrator in 1274. In 1275–1276 Robert was granted the castle and town of Orford in Suffolk, which became the family seat, and in 1276 Robert was the rather unpopular Justiciar of Ireland.[49] A writ in 1281 appoints Stephen Fulburn, Bishop of Waterford, as justiciar in Robert's place as Robert 'by reason of his infirmity, cannot perform the duty'[50], so he may have been unwell for a few years before his death in 1298. His son Robert (1279–1316) further increased the family standing and possessions, helped by marrying the wealthy co-heiress Cicely de Valoines, a noble Suffolk family descended from Norman nobility and given lands by William the Conqueror after 1066[51]. He died quite young, aged approximately thirty-seven, and his firstborn son, William, had predeceased him. His second but eldest surviving son, Robert, was born 9 August 1298 and received his father's inheritance in May 1318, where it states he was under-age (probably around nineteen years old). He had been a ward in the household of Edward II, becoming a knight of the household between 1318 and 1319.[52]

Robert Ufford (1298–1369) was also a tenant of Thomas of Brotherton, being in his retinue in 1322 preparing for war in Scotland[53], as well as appearing in the household of Edward III in 1328[54]. Robert continued to serve in Thomas' household as he witnessed some of Thomas' charters in the 1330s, including bearing witness to Alice of Norfolk's marriage arrangements with Montagu, which must have been a very solemn affair as the great earls of Warenne, Arundel and Warwick were also present, among others[55].

In the October 1330 Nottingham Castle coup, which saw Queen Isabella's military leader and possible lover Roger Mortimer arrested and Edward III take his rightful place as king, one of the close-knit members who stormed the castle with the leader William Montagu was Robert Ufford. Robert played a vital role in the success of the coup. In February 1331 his involvement is proved as we see him being given a general pardon by Edward III 'for the deaths of Hugh de Turpliton, knight, and Richard de Monemuth killed whilst resisting the arrest of Roger de Mortuo Mari [Mortimer] at Nottingham Castle.'[56] In 1337 Robert was made an earl, along with William Montagu, and in 1338 he was with the king in Antwerp, as was Edward Montagu. Robert had, by November 1324, married Margaret of Norwich, and as we have seen, two of their sons would marry two of Alice's daughters.

The Norfolk Plantagenets and the Uffords would have been very familiar with each other with an association going back quite a few years.

Alice's Grandchildren

Alice and Edward's two eldest children died young, their third child and second daughter, Elizabeth, despite two marriages, died without issue, and Maud had entered an ecclesiastical life. Therefore, only Joan, the youngest child and fourth daughter, produced any grandchildren.

Joan and William Ufford had five children in total, four sons and a daughter, which sounds hopeful of a dynasty and the continuation of Alice's lineage. Joan was pregnant either just before or just after her fourteenth birthday, with Robert, the firstborn child, son and heir of William. Robert was married by 28 October 1371 to Eleanor Fitz-Alan, daughter of Richard, the son and heir apparent to the Earl of Arundel[57]. However, it appears Robert had died by 1374, as we see by an entry in the Court of Common Pleas naming Joan's second son, Thomas, as son and heir. In June 1374 a plea of covenant was heard whereby a certain William de Huntyngfeld (Huntingfield) would revert certain land and manors to the heirs of William Ufford, 2nd Earl of Suffolk, and upon William's death, to his son, Thomas, and to his male heirs. In the default of heirs of Thomas, next in line would be Thomas' brother, also William, and in default of male heirs in that line, next would be the younger brother to Thomas and William, Edward Ufford.[58]

In 1375 an inquisition into William Ufford, 2nd Earl of Suffolk, granting manors without licence, held by right of his wife, Joan, shows that Robert, William and Joan's son and heir, and Robert's wife, Eleanor FitzAlan, had both died by this time, without issue. In the August of 1375 Joan had also died 'without an heir of her body' meaning all of her remaining children had also died – all of her sons within the last ten months since they were mentioned in records in June 1374, and also a daughter, Margaret Ufford, alive in early 1375 when aid for her marriage was levied[59]. Seven years later, on 15 February 1382, Ufford was ascending the stairs at Westminster (possibly at the doorway of St Stephen's Chapel) after being elected to represent the knights of his lands in Norfolk and Suffolk, when he collapsed and died instantly. According to the chronicler Thomas Walsingham, Ufford had 'entered the court at Westminster in merry mood and not feeling at all ill ... not only all the nobles of the kingdom but also the middle classes and even the poor felt great consternation at his sudden death ... as he had shown himself a lovable person to all men'.[60]

Despite a second marriage, William Ufford died with no heirs, having no issue from either of his two marriages, and the earldom died with him, until four years later when it was granted to the de Pole family by King Richard II. With the death of Joan, aged twenty-six, and her five children predeceasing her and her husband, this was the end of Alice's inheritance, which reverted to her sister, Margaret of Norfolk. The plague had struck again in 1375 so it is within reason to assume that this could have been the cause of wiping out an entire family in a relatively short space of time. Joan and her husband were buried at Campsey Priory, Suffolk, the wealthiest priory in the Norwich Diocese, and where the Uffords had their private burial chamber, consisting of Purbeck marble tombs, near the south aisle of the choir.[61] Campsey Priory had been established c.1195 by the ancestors of William's grandmother, Cicely Valoines, who bought it to the Uffords via marriage. The death of Alice's final child, Maud, in 1393 marked the end of Alice of Norfolk's blood lineage.[62]

Towards the end of 1349 we see Edward Montagu turning repeatedly to crime and intimidation and becoming notorious across East Anglia. On 6 November 1349 Edward Montagu is being sued for monies owed to Berard Albret, a cadet member of the powerful Albret family from Gascony who supported the English in the Hundred Years War, with Berard being an English commander. This is also the same family that Alice of Norfolk's young cousin, Margaret of Kent, daughter of Edmund, Thomas' younger brother, would marry into. Although Berard had died in 1346, the executor of his will, John Gastinelli, appointed attorneys before the king to sue for monies owed by Edward pursuant to the statue of merchants and a vintner was also present.[63] Then, on 16 October 1350, a commission of oyer and terminer (criminal trial) was raised in Westminster by Margery, the widow of Baron William de Ros (sometimes spelt Roos), herself a distant relation of Alice. Edward Montagu was accused, along with nineteen other named men, as well as 'others', of taking cattle from her land and driving said cattle to places unknown, thus preventing her from recovering them and her land rendered unworkable. Her men and her servants were also assaulted and had been out of her service for a while. Amongst these named men, two are priests of Edward's, one is a bailiff, as well as a man named John Dunche. We also have a John de Hales and Randolf de Hales accused – the Hales family were Alice's maternal kin, her mother being Alice Hales, daughter of a Norfolk coroner. This attack, whilst not too unusual in the dire economic climate of the fourteenth century, comes across as mob-handed and violent. The highest-ranking name listed is Edward Montagu, so whilst it maybe conjecture, it is within reason to imagine him as the ringleader. It also shows how hard times might have been; the plague had ravaged all of England the year before and it changed agrarian farming forever. Arable land diminished in importance and the trend towards cattle and stock rearing, dairy farming and the expense of herdsmen, one can see that cattle was extremely valuable in this time.[64]

Which begs the question: where did Alice's wealth go? Of course, the natural disasters would have contributed, but Alice had been a wealthy co-heiress. By the mid-1300s over seventy per cent of crime was theft, usually linked to poverty; the shock of the plague epidemic in 1348–9 led to a death rate of fifty per cent and coincided with a deterioration in the global climate, as discussed earlier. The second epidemic of 1361–2 had a lesser death rate but contributed to the ongoing social and economic dire straits of the fourteenth century, including a shortage of workers, rising prices, and general depopulation, with Norfolk suffering considerably with the latter.[65]

However, in terms of managing land and surviving these catastrophes, it is interesting to note that of all the Suffolk castles, Bungay had the deepest well for fresh water, an exceptional rich environment to grow food, and mature woodland to support pigs.[66] In fact, Bungay Manor had a history of generating approximately seventy per cent of its income from non-agricultural purposes, such as market stalls, rents and courts. Tenants rented grazing rights and the castle garden itself supplied fruit trees, and tenants brewed malt and sowed barley and wheat for use at Framlingham as well as Bungay. Workers included swineherds, ploughmen and dairy keepers.[67] However, the famine, floods and drought would have had a major knock-on effect to its income, and it can be of no coincidence that Edward's criminal activities run parallel with this social-economic depression that broke societal norms from 1349 onwards.[68]

On Sunday, 19 June 1351, when Alice and Edward's youngest child, Joan, was two years old, a tragedy unfolded in the family home of Bungay Castle. Alice was beaten almost to death by her husband. *The Complete Peerage*, Volume 9, p.85, quoting Ancient Indictments no.114 *m*.13, states that:

Itemqe le dit Mons Edward William Dunch et Thomas persone del eglise de Kelleshale a force et armes et feloneusement baterount Alice fille atThomas de Brotherton cosyne a tire seignour le Roy et compaigne au dit Mons Edward 21Bungeye ceste assauoir le Dimeigne procheyn apres la feste de seynt Botolf en laan du regne le Roy qore est vynt et quynte, de qele baterye la dite Alice langwyt malade tancqe a la mort et ele murrust deynz laan et le jour.

Item, that the said Sir Edward, William Dunch, and Thomas, parson of the church of Kelsale, with force and arms feloniously beat [baterount] Alice, daughter of Thomas of Brotherton, cousin of our lord the king, and wife of the said Sir Edward, at Bungay, that is, on the Sunday next after the feast of Saint Botolf in the twenty-fifth year of the reign of the present king, of which assault [baterye] the said Alice fell ill unto death and she died within the year and the day.

Translation by kind courtesy of Kathryn Warner.

St Botolph was a Saxon noble living in the seventh century who founded a monastery in Suffolk. His feast day is 17 June, and this fell on a Friday in 1351 (the Julian calendar was in use at this time). Thus, the Sunday after would be 19 June, the day on which Alice was beaten so severely by her husband and two of his retainers that she never regained her health. From this, and from various chancery records, a timeline can be established from the day of Alice's attack to the time of her death.

Five months after the attack, on 14 November 1351, there is an entry in the Fine Rolls for William de Middleton, escheator in the counties of Norfolk and Suffolk, regarding Alice of Norfolk. An escheator was a royal officer responsible for overseeing the reversion of lands and property of the deceased back to the lord or Crown; in this case back to the king as Alice, although technically her husband's property, was the tenant-in-chief. Alice's death must have then been reported to officials approximately five months after the attack. However, an addendum was added after stating that the escheator 'vacated because it is testified that Alice is alive'.[69]

Also in November 1351, the king's serjeant at arms, Richard de Bosevill, was to take the two underage daughters and heirs of Alice into the care of their paternal grandmother, Elizabeth Montagu (nee Montfort), the widow of William Montagu and Edward's mother.[70] We know that Elizabeth, Maud and Joan were alive in 1359, so Elizabeth may have already been living in the household of her husband, Walter Ufford, when her mother was attacked in 1351. The two daughters mentioned in this order must have been Maud, aged around four or five years, and Joan, aged two years, at the time of their mother's attack. Interestingly, on 28 November 1351 Edward Montagu had to appoint an attorney for his interests in Ireland: 'Edward de Monte Acuto, staying in England, has letters nominating John de Podesye as his attorney in Ireland for two years.'[71] It is therefore possible that Edward had been ordered not to leave the country after the attack on Alice, and, with the exception of being in the retinue of William, 2nd Earl of Salisbury, in 1356 and leaving for Gascony with the Black Prince, it does appear he doesn't travel abroad again, although he was still being summoned to Parliament until just a few months before his death in 1361.[72]

Alice was, therefore, still alive in November 1351, but though as it had been originally reported that she had died. Looking at this from a medical point of view, this is very much a sign that Alice's condition drastically deteriorated. Two months later, on 15 January 1352, the sheriff of Norfolk was ordered to pay Mary, the widowed Countess of Norfolk who was also Alice's stepmother, arrears from Norwich Castle with 'the assent of John de Segrave and Margaret his wife, the earl's eldest daughter and heir, and of Edward de Monte Acuto and Alice his wife, the earl's second daughter and heir'.[73] It is highly unlikely that Alice assented, as, a mere two weeks later, on 30 January, the escheator was again ordered to deal with her lands. This time there was no addendum, so one can safely say Alice had died.[74]

Less than two weeks later, on 10 February 1352, William de Middleton was ordered 'not to intermeddle with the lands which Edward Montagu holds by the law of England by reasons of the death of Alice his wife ... restoring to him any which he has taken,' as the king had taken homage (feudal acknowledgment) from Edward when they were in Flanders, probably around 1340, for 'all the lands which he and Alice held in chief of her inheritance, by reason of their common offspring.' A few days later, on 15 February 1352, the marriage arrangements of Alice's daughters, although pertaining to the king, were granted to their father, Edward, by 'special grace' of the king.[75]

The Complete Peerage cites Ancient Indictments No.114 for its record of Alice's attack. This means Alice's murder was heard in a senior criminal court, The King's Bench, and if not in the presence of the king himself, it would have been within his immediate jurisdiction.[76] There is no record of Edward Montagu suffering any inconvenience concerning his wife's death, a most violent attack committed by him and two of his retainers. In fact, he seems almost placated, and although the husbands of deceased female heiresses, tenants-in-chief, still had control of lands and property until their own death, none appears to be taken from Edward Montagu, including the marriage of his daughters, usually the remit of the king in this case because, let's not forget, Alice is a first cousin of the king, a Plantagenet, and the daughter of an earl. However, she was also Edward's property by law.

Why did Edward attack his wife so? Why did it take three of them, using weapons, to attack a high-ranking noblewoman? Unfortunately, due to lack of information, one needs to use some conjecture and supposition by looking at the facts that are known.

Even in the context of medieval England, the attack on Alice still seems particularly violent. Domestic violence was an accepted societal norm during this period of history, with 'physical correction of wives' and a degree of physical force being expected within a marriage.[77] Indeed, medieval domestic violence was considered integral to an orderly household and wasn't considered unusual, barring extreme circumstances such as murder. It was perfectly legal to beat your wife. Royal courts did not utilise any time or administration on domestic violence unless it pertained to murder; ecclesiastical courts saw domestic violence as being symptomatic of bigger issues of marital strife, such as adultery or desertion, and focused on what we would recognise today as marriage guidance counselling.[78]

A 2001 study of fourteenth-century Coroner's Rolls regarding domestic violence shows that out of fifty-two cases of spousal abuse, forty-one of those resulted in uxoricide (wife-killing). The husband was almost always the main suspect, with thirty-seven of those forty-one uxoricides thought to be committed as a solitary act by the husband; only three of those note a conclusion of acquittal. The Coroner's Rolls were written in a 'terse, unrevealing and formulaic' manner, which is what we find when questioning Alice's fate.[79] From this, it is easy to see how Edward Montagu crossed a boundary, even by fourteenth-century standards, by causing the death of his wife, Alice, in an episode of extreme domestic violence. Not only had he beaten her to the extreme, he had two accomplices, unusual in itself.

One of Edward's accomplices in this attack on Alice was, in fact, supposedly a holy man, the local parson of Kelsale, Suffolk (also spelt Keleshale, Kellishale, Kellesale in documents), called Thomas. Eight months before the attack on Alice, when Edward and others were accused of cattle-stealing in October 1350, one of those men with Edward was Thomas *Edwardesprestmontagu* (Edward's priest). Could this be the same Thomas? At the time of the attack on Alice, the parson of Kelsale was William Butteveleyn (Botevilelyn).[80] In November 1352, ten months after Alice's death, Butteveleyn resigned Kelsale and moved to the rectory at Tunstall (south of Bungay), which had been vacated by a priest named Thomas atte Gate who was then instituted at Kelsale; Butteveleyn and Gate basically swapped parishes and both had the same patron, Edward Montagu. Thomas had only been instituted as a priest at Tunstall since 19 January 1352 upon the resignation of William Hales, who also had the patronage of Edward, and who was highly likely to have been Alice's kin. The date of Hales' resignation and Thomas's placement was 19 January 1352, when Alice would have been in her last few days of life, if not already dead; all that the records show is that she had died by 30 January. William Hales had been the priest at Tunstall since March 1346 but had resigned the benefice with no reason given. Usually it is to move on to another parish, but any forwarding activity is missing from the Bishop of Norwich's register for William Hales. Using pure conjecture, his resignation may have been as a result of Alice's attack.[81]

Interestingly, the Bishop of Norwich's register shows that between 1346 and 1353 Edward Montagu made sixteen institutions as patron of his and Alice's advowsons, meaning Edward and Alice were exercising their right to appoint a member of the clergy to a vacant ecclesiastical office, such as a vicar or priest and relevant property/income that would come with the post. These advowsons, seen as property, were inherited from Alice's father, Thomas, Earl of Norfolk; eight of these appointments were in July 1349 (and we have already seen how this was the peak of the plague in East Anglia and the effect it had on the clergy). Edward Montagu was at various locations in Norfolk and Suffolk when the institutions were confirmed in the register, all except one, on 19 January 1352, when it seems he was likely in London. Is it possible Alice had died by the 19 January and Edward was in London attending his indictment for her death? Why else would he be so far away when she was dying or had just died?[82]

Thomas atte Gate had been instituted at Kelsale and all this was confirmed by Edward Montagu on 16 November 1352. Thankfully, William Bateman, Bishop of Norwich, kept his registers as up to date as possible during the time of the plague, but record keeping was affected to a degree; Thomas atte Gate could have easily been priest of

Kelsale before this official record. Being a patron of the clergy meant Alice of Norfolk and her sister had inherited the financial business of wealthy advowsons - which could be sold as an asset if needed as well as generating income such as tithes - from their father. In fact, Alice – and therefore Edward Montagu – inherited sixteen advowsons, including two priories, Bungay and the smaller Weybridge in Norfolk, with two of the churches being Tunstall and Kelsale.[83]

Also in the cattle-stealing complaint in October 1350 was John Dunch, and in the assault on Alice there was mentioned a William Dunch. Local history records show Dunch[e] to be a common surname in Suffolk at the time. There is also Dunche's Lane, an unmade track connecting two lanes in a village in Suffolk between Creeting St Mary and Earl Soham (Stonham), part of the Brotherton inheritance and where a certain Thomas Dunche was rector of the Creeting All Saints church from 1427 to 1447. Also stemming from this period is Dunche's Charity, still distributing to those in need today although the beginnings of the charity are unknown. However, being originally appropriated to the poor of Creeting All Saints church, the charity must be named after Thomas Dunche, the rector. Perhaps William Dunch was the bad apple.[84]

Therefore, this is possibly the family of the thuggish William Dunch, who was pardoned in June 1361 for his part in the assault on Alice as well as other felonies and trespasses such as stealing from Bungay Priory, cattle stealing and bribing victims for return of their goods, 'for having taken by force sixteen cows, worth 10 marks, from James, prior of Thetford Monachorum, and impounded them until the prior bound himself in 10l. to Edward de Mountagu for their deliverance', as well as many accounts of theft, all because of his 'good service in the war of France in the company of Sir William de Felton'.[85] Felton, in the king's retinue, had had a small retinue of his own – three knights and nine esquires – in the Battle of Crécy in 1346. Dunch was not a knight so he must have been in Crécy as an esquire, a knight's assistance or shield-bearer, who would usually be member of the gentry class.[86] The timing of his pardon is interesting as at this point, June 1361, Edward Montagu would have been ill or at least known he was dying, as we can see from his Inquisition Post Mortem dated 14 July 1361.

Did Dunch receive the majority of the punishment for the attack on Alice so that Edward didn't? It was not unusual for those serving in the king's armies, be they a man of God or not, to be pardoned for criminal activities, including rape, pillage and general thuggery. Whilst abhorrent to us today, gentry and magnate crime needs to be understood in the context of the fourteenth century. Warring political factions due to local and national unrest, legal disputes between noble families – usually power struggles, social-economic hardship and many people often in rural isolation, miles from towns and sheriffs. Whilst gentry and magnate crime wasn't necessarily considered lawless by contemporaries in the fourteenth century, the Indictments and sometimes flowery writing of the Chronicles of the day, may distort the realities of living in such difficult times.[87] Although the account of Edward's attack on his wife is hardly flowery; more brutal, to the point, and factual.

In the realms of knighthood, we have a certain Sir John Moleyns of Buckinghamshire who served loyally in the retinue of Edward's brother, the Earl of Salisbury, William Montagu. Moleyns had a list of murder, cattle-stealing and theft attributed to him, which would eventually be his undoing, and he died in Cambridge Castle in 1360. Roger Hales, son of Sir John Hales, Alice's maternal kin and most likely the same person mentioned in the cattle-stealing episode of October 1350, was previously pardoned in June 1346 for the rape of Alice de Layton,[88] at the request of Robert Ufford, Earl of Suffolk and the future father-in-law of Alice's daughters, Elizabeth and Joan. A month later, in July 1346, Roger Hales was pardoned again after being indicted of 'having ravished and deflowered Alice, his own daughter, whereof she died, of having assaulted Alice wife of Robert de Hales and Walter her son ... of having entered the house of Walter Red of Hales and assaulted him.'[89] Alice would have been aware of this.

In 1354 Thomas de Lisle, Bishop of Ely, who had taken the post of bishop after the death of Edward's brother, Simon Montagu, was accused of attacking Lady Wake, widow of Thomas Wake, a cousin of the king and of Alice. The king did investigate this, and during the proceedings there came to light a string of corruption, murder, arson and theft felonies over his eleven years as bishop, as well as accusations of running criminal gang activities – including priests – across East Anglia.[90]

There appears to be no distinction for violence regarding those in the lower echelons of society. In 1350 there is record of a certain John Lavenham, Nicholas Bolton and John Watham, all of whom were pardoned for the rape of Eleanor de Merton owing to their good service to the king in Calais.[91] Geoffrey de Marleputte, in the retinue of the Earl of Warwick, was pardoned in 1361 for murder, robbery, escaping prison, trespass and theft from the Archbishop of Canterbury's tenants in the agricultural and industrial rich villages of Harrow, Hayes and Ruislip in Middlesex.[92] Having these men in aristocratic retinues appears not to adversely affect anyone's career. In his 2014 study, Matthew Thompson states that 'The sheer number of such men pardoned, and that is only those pardons enrolled, implies that great numbers of men saw military service as an effective means of avoiding paying the price for their crimes.' Which puts Edward Montagu, who most likely served with some of those mentioned, acting with expected norms within his milieu.[93]

However, although all this recorded history gives a backdrop of society that Alice and Edward would have known, it still doesn't explain the seemingly murderous attack of Alice. What can be assumed from this? One could argue that Alice, as was the law of the time (and abhorrent as it sounds to us today), was being 'physically corrected' by her husband and simply fell and hit her head, for example. After all, there are no records throughout their lengthy union and rather fertile marriage of similar occurrences. A plausible explanation could be that Alice had given birth to yet another daughter or miscarried a son (not recorded anywhere so unlikely any child did not survive) when Edward's only son and heir had more than likely already died by this point in time, exacerbating the fact that as part of the elite, he had no male heir, a very important facet of medieval nobility.

The incident could have been the result of escalating variables, bearing in mind the socio-economic disasters Alice and Edward were living with. Was he frightened of losing everything due to the economic, social and religious consequences of the time, which affected nobility and peasantry alike, and Alice bore the brunt of this? The plague was episodic during the fourteenth century and was something to fear greatly at that time – it had most likely taken his son and heir, and firstborn daughter. After all, society felt that even God had deserted them in this time as archbishops and clergy also fell victim, with three archbishops dying within a year:

> God is deaf now-a-days and deigneth not to hear us,
> And prayers have no power the Plague to stay.[94]

Was Alice in the wrong place at the wrong time? Was she on the receiving end of his anger on this occasion? Was he haunted by his humble beginnings of being a younger son, climbing the social ladder to become a knight then marrying a member of the royal family, and did this suddenly overwhelm him because they were suffering financially? Had Alice stood up to him for what could be a myriad of reasons? However, going by the description of the incident whereby 'with force and arms feloniously beat Alice, daughter of Thomas of Brotherton', it appears to be a much more volatile, enraged reaction to something recent, a knee-jerk response to something critical – perhaps the death of his son wasn't caused by the plague, but a more recent illness and Edward's reaction was to blame his wife? They used force, they used weapons, and there were three of them. Although a husband could beat his wife, one has to wonder how much Alice fought back if his cowardly accomplices also beat her.

It will probably never be known why it happened, but it must be considered that Edward did not mean to murder Alice. It would have been easy to kill her there and then, but he and his retainers did not, and they were not to know if she would survive and be a credible witness. And judging by the notorious reputation Edward and his men had in

Bungay and its environs, any household members would remain silent through fear of their lord. Was she protecting her two small daughters, Maud and Joan, who were still living at Bungay at the time of the attack? Although Alice didn't die five months later in November, as was first thought, there is no record of the two small children being returned to her, or Edward, which shows Alice was not capable of childcare, either hands-on or overseeing one of her household. The children, at such young ages, were obviously considered safer away from Bungay Castle at that time. The last line in the *Complete Peerage* statement regarding the incident – 'the said Alice fell ill unto death and she died within the year and the day' – shows us that Alice never recovered in any way from her attack. Therefore, she appears to have had a long, lingering death over the course of seven months, possibly deteriorating after five months when it was wrongly reported she had passed away. Looking at it again from a medical point of view, Alice may have sustained severe wounds that didn't heal and led to septicaemia or a localised infection of some sort. The situation could also be indicative of severe head injuries, possibly a coma, but most certainly brain damage. Seven months, with no modern-day assistive intensive care to help, is a relatively long time to sustain a cardiovascular system before it became too much. Depending on her injuries, and even if Alice had regained consciousness, her swallowing, breathing, nutrition and hydration would all be impaired[95].

Four months after Alice's death, Edward continued his law-breaking. In May 1352 records show that Edward, along with a certain Henry le Bakere and John le Botillier, as well as 'others', broke into the premises of William de la Marche, in Dichyngham, Norfolk, stealing goods and displaying such threatening behaviour that William dared not stay at his own property and his servants were too scared to serve him, rendering him with no income[96]. Edward Montagu must have been terrifying. Perversely, these traits, whilst abhorrent to us today, would have been extremely useful in the wars of the fourteenth century. Edward fought in Crécy, and more than likely made a good soldier with his capability of violent conduct, and one has to wonder if he hadn't married Alice

Plantagenet of Norfolk, and all that she bought with her, he would have made a good mercenary.

He did, however, continue to be summoned to Parliament, and in 1354, regarding appointing proxies to treat with France, he is addressed as *dominus de Bungey* (Lord of Bungay) with other magnates such as Thomas Braose, *dominus de Bosham*, who had married the young widow of Edward's brother-in-law, Alice's brother, Edward of Norfolk, and gained the wealthy lands of Bosham, at a loss to Brotherton.[97] In 1356 he was appointed custodian of the Norfolk coastal area, along with others, including John of Norwich, whose sister Margaret had married Robert Ufford, Earl of Suffolk, and who was mother-in-law of Edward's daughters, Elizabeth and Joan, and John Reppes, whose family had also been in Thomas of Brotherton's affinity. Edward Montagu was actually a substitute for John Bardolf, a Norfolk knight, who, for 'certain reasons', could not perform his duties. On this occasion, Edward III greeted him thus: 'KING, to his beloved and faithful Edward of Monte Acuto, greetings'.[98] But, as previously mentioned, although Edward Montagu was in the retinue of his nephew William, 2nd Earl of Salisbury in 1356, he appears not to have gone abroad on business after the death of Alice and in the years leading up to his death in July 1361. Perhaps he had been ordered, or at least advised, not to leave the country for his role in Alice's death? Edward Montagu had married again by at least 1358, to a lady known only as Joan. He had another daughter by Joan, born c.1359 (she was aged two at his death and will be looked at later in the book). He also had another son, also named Edward, by Joan, who was only seven weeks old when Montagu died in July 1361, and who followed his father to the grave only a couple of months later.[99]

According to a rather vague, modern-day online resource (findagrave. com), Alice was supposedly buried in the church of St Thomas in Bungay, although no reference or source is given to corroborate this. Today's Victorian church of St Edmund's stands on the site.[100] The church of St Thomas was next to that of St Mary, known in Alice's time as the church of the Holy Cross, and both were of Saxon origin (two of five Saxon churches recorded in Bungay in the Domesday Book of 1086).[101] In c.1160, on the land around these two churches, Bungay Priory was founded for an order of Benedictine nuns by Countess Gundreda, the widow of Roger Bigod, Earl of Norfolk, and her second husband, Roger Glanville. A generous endowment of confirmation was given in a charter by Henry II in 1176,[102] and a charter reaffirming this and other benefactors was issued on 18 March 1235 by Henry III.[103] Gundreda had died by 1208, as had her son and heir, Hugh Bigod, as we see the younger of her two sons, William Bigod, suing for rights of a watermill in nearby Wainford. Glanville had close ties with the counties of Norfolk and Suffolk, coming from a family of sheriffs, and his brother, Ranulf, was Chief Justiciar of England. Roger Glanville was quite possibly the great-grandson of a certain Robert Glanville, mentioned in the Domesday Book as holding lands including Suffolk, and his family founded the Suffolk priories of Butley (1170s) and Leiston (1180s), both of which were granted to the Uffords in 1337. The date of Gundreda's marriage to Glanville is uncertain but he was on Crusade with Richard I in 1190 and had died by 1197/8 when Gundreda paid a fine to the king so she would not have to marry against her will in future. They had no issue.[104]

Although the church of St Thomas in Bungay was appropriated to the priory early on, not much else is known or recorded about it, including exactly where it was, but it was still being used in 1500 and most likely fell with the priory at the Dissolution in 1536. There are also records of a chapel in the same area dedicated to St Mary Magdalene. Some attempt at restoration was attempted in 1541 with a description of clay walls and a thatched roof and in 1565 it became a grammar school. In 1580 the school was moved to a new site, burnt down in the Great Fire of Bungay in 1688 and rebuilt where it was until 1925.[105]

St Mary's, on the other hand, was not only a mere appendage but was rebuilt over the Saxon building to become the priory church of Bungay Priory. After the Dissolution, St Mary's became the local parish church, being retired in 1977 and now looked after by The Churches Conservation Trust.[106] A third nearby church, the oldest building in Bungay, Holy Trinity, is still standing, with its late Saxon stone tower and with the arms of Montagu and Brotherton inlaid in the tower. Considering this, and the fact that Bungay Priory is considered the burial place of its founder, Countess Gundreda, it is highly likely that Alice Plantagenet of Norfolk, Lady Montagu, was laid to rest somewhere here. It is doubtful that the noble Alice was buried in the surrounding areas of St Thomas or the small chapel of St Mary Magadelene. The priory would have originally extended from Cross Street down to Olland Street and the south-west corner of Holy Trinity churchyard, with the priory precinct lying between St Mary's Street and Trinity Street (see map, Appendix 2). Although the few remains of the priory can be seen today in the churchyard of St Mary's, as well as parts of the surrounding wall, this area would have originally been a processional walkway to the Holy Trinity church. Bungay Priory precinct originally extended from the south of St Mary's church (the north of the church was for the townspeople) and was probably not used as a place for general burials until after the Dissolution. Thereafter, the lost priory precinct around St Mary's was overgrown and not enclosed until 1791, being completely enclosed by 1798, although Trinity Street was beginning to take form in 1764. According to the local historian Ethel Mann (1861–1947), when the grass track area – informally known as Lady's Walk – was dug up to lay Trinity Street in the late eighteenth century, many skeletons were found 'going in all directions'.[107] Alfred Suckling, the clergyman and Suffolk historian, writing in 1846, states that the ruins seen in St Mary's churchyard, some of which can still be seen today, contain the ruined chancel and the remains of a chapel abutting it, quoting the *Inquisitio ad Quod Damnum* in 1373 as finding provision 'for a chaplain to perform divine service in the chapel of the Virgin Mary at the priory of Bungay.' Suckling quotes the full text: '*Rex concedat Rogero Rose et Johan Dunkon quod ipsi 2 cotag: 55 acr: terr: 8 acr: prat: et dimid: alneti cum pertinent in Ilketilishall, Metyngham, Flixton, et Dychyngham; et Rogero Longe Personæ eccliæ de Homersfield, quod ipsi unum messuag: 30 acr: terr: 2 ac: prati in Southelmham dare possint, ad inveniendum unum capellanum divina duobus diebus qualibet septimana in capellâ beatæ Maciæ prioratus prædæ, pro animabus &c. celebratur: in perpet: et præd: mess: et ten: valent p: an: 24 solidos'.* An *Inquisitio ad Quod Damnum* was a request to the Crown to alienate land, usually to religious houses or request a market and a translated, shortened version of the above unfortunately doesn't confirm the request for a chaplain for two days a week.[108]

Mann, writing in 1934, also noted that in 1373/4 a provision was made for a chaplain to perform divine service and for money to burn candles in the chapel of St Mary at Bungay Priory, and goes further to say that this was considered the place where the tomb of Countess Gundreda, the founder, was laid to rest. Mann doesn't corroborate this fact but does state in her book that she had access to original manuscripts and endeavoured to obtain 'from every available resource, an additional information that may render [the book] more reliable'.[109] Indeed, the *Valor Ecclesiasticus* of 1534, a valuation of all the churches in England and Wales commissioned by Henry VIII to see what monasteries to close down (his Dissolution started two years later in 1536), states that Bungay Priory had a value of £72 (approximately £32,000 today) and that 'The sum of 12s 4d was annually expended in this monastery in alms to the poor, on the anniversary of Gundreda, countess of Norfolk, who was considered the foundress, and also for wax lights to burn around her tomb on the same day.'[110] Mann is correct that Gundreda's tomb is thereabouts, and most likely where Suckling noted it to be. After the Dissolution, the famous Bungay fire of March 1688, which added to the priory's destruction, and led to stone being taken for local buildings over the years, caused many burial sites to be lost, including the likely tomb of Alice. However, it would be nice to think she wasn't disturbed too much in death as she had been at the end of her short life.[111]

Medieval women were often considered chattels or possessions of their husbands. Indeed, it was a world dominated by a patriarchal society and women did become their husband's property when married, but they also held their own power. Alice's own sister, Margaret, defied their cousin Edward III, not just once but twice, and successfully managed her own estates, showing us that these women were often highly intelligent and capable, operating successfully within accepted societal parameters. Researching further, one will find greatness in the likes of

Nicholaa de la Haye, Maud Broase and Alice's own stepmother, Mary Broase, Countess of Norfolk, with regard to their intelligence, courage and determination.[112] Eleanor de Montfort, sister of Henry III and wife to Simon de Montfort, was considered so spirited and forceful she was reprimanded by a Franciscan friar, Adam Marsh, to 'act in a spirit of moderation'. She didn't and her household accounts show she was frequently in charge of all matters.[113] Who knows what greatness Alice might have gone on to do if she had lived long enough and not faded into time? What impact might she have had on her children growing up? And how would she have compared to her sister, or even her cousin, Joan of Kent? In the eyes of the law and the Church, Alice of Norfolk may have been the property of Edward Montagu, and thus it would have been difficult to be held accountable for her death, but he must have known that his position, and his place in society, was all thanks to Alice, not himself.

Chapter 2

The Powerful Granddaughter, Margaret of Norfolk

Alice's elder sister, Margaret, was born c.1322, likely the first child and daughter of Thomas, Earl of Norfolk and his wife, Alice Hales.[1] Alice and Margaret also had a brother, Edward of Norfolk, but he had died young, at least by 1334, and he will be discussed further in the book. As with much of the Brotherton family, Margaret's early life is vague, although as time went on she turned out to be a rather formidable Plantagenet, the common family trait. This included ignoring etiquette of the day and completely ignoring the laws of her cousin, King Edward III, when she travelled abroad to ask the Pope to grant her a divorce from her first husband, Sir John Segrave. Although the quest for a divorce was unsuccessful, after Segrave's death she remarried Sir Walter Mauny (also known as Manny) almost immediately and without royal permission. Margaret had issue from both unions but subsequently went on to outlive not just all of her immediate family but almost everyone around her.

In March 1327, for his (unspecified) service to Queen Isabella, the young King Edward III granted Thomas Brotherton the wardship and marriage rights of the ten-year-old John Segrave.[2] Although Edward III was announced king just two months previous to this, in January 1327, this time period was in the regency of Edward's mother, Queen Isabella, and her aide, Roger Mortimer, until Edward III overthrew them in 1330.[3] Thomas subsequently went onto betroth his elder daughter, Margaret, to John, and they were married c.1335, which is not surprisingly really, as one would most likely want to keep the value of a large landowner in the family.[4]

Who was John Segrave? He was the 4th Lord Segrave (b.1315–d.1353). His family came from a long line of sheriffs, justiciars and landowners in Segrave (now known as Seagrave) in Lincolnshire and Warwickshire and the family rose prominently in wealth and power under Henry III. John's great-grandfather, Nicholas (d.1295) was the first Lord Segrave and was a squire in 1257 in the household of Prince Edward, who would become Edward I, father of Thomas Brotherton and grandfather of Margaret.[5] Nicholas died sometime before November 1295 and his eldest son and heir, John, had died by October 1325.[6] John's eldest son and heir, another Stephen Segrave, was Constable of the Tower of London in August 1323 during the escape of Roger Mortimer, who would eventually overthrow Edward II (in conjunction with Edward's wife, Queen Isabella, who is discussed in a later chapter). The deputy constable of the Tower in August 1323 was a man called Gerard Alspaye and it was he who aided in the sedation of Segrave and the other guards, enabling him to take Mortimer through the kitchens to a waiting rope ladder leading down to a boat on the Thames, where Mortimer sympathisers aided the escape. Stephen Segrave is noted as being seriously ill from the effects of being sedated and could no longer perform his task of Constable.[7] What could have knocked out the guards so effectively that Mortimer, such a high-profile prisoner of the day, could escape? Knowledge of plants and herbs would have been much more common than it is today and the methods of rendering a person unconscious before surgery, for example, go back to Roman times. Early medical texts such as *leechbooks* contained many recipes from the Anglo-Saxon era. In 1992 an extensive study of twelfth-to-fifteenth-century texts discovered a common recipe amongst the *leechbooks* called *dwale*. This was a common mixture of the era, consisting of three deadly poisons, henbane, opium and hemlock, all of which can prove fatal in the smallest of doses – not forgetting the alcohol content of the wine in which the sedative was administered. The fact that Stephen Segrave is noted as being seriously ill indicates the possibility that he may have had a reaction or ingested an amount that would have caused quite severe respiratory paralysis.[8] Of course, it could have been a mix of anything, but it is interesting to note of the commonly available *dwale* drink of the era.

Stephen's son, John, came into his inheritance aged just ten years old due to his grandfather and namesake John Segrave dying in October 1325 and his father, Stephen, eldest son of John Senior, dying very shortly after, sometime before 12 December 1325, with John named as his heir. He was in Thomas of Brotherton's wardship from 1325 until he came of age in 1336.[9]

It is well documented that Margaret of Norfolk was not happily married to Segrave. In March 1344 we see John Segrave declaring a charter concerning arrangements for his and Margaret's separate households, witnessed by the Earl of Arundel 'and other nobles', showing they were living separate lives at this point.[10] In January 1350 Edward III had prohibited all travel overseas, but in October that same year, Margaret defied Edward III by travelling abroad to seek the Pope's permission to divorce John Segrave, travelling across the channel in a barge called *le Faucoun* (the master of said barge was a man call Nicholas Lorecok, who used the boat without knowledge of the owner, William de Denum). The writ of August 1351 goes on to say that 'she was met at night by Thomas Barbour, servant of Sir Walter de Mauny, by whom he was appointed to superintend the crossing; he broke his lantern with his foot so that he could not exercise his office.'[11] Margaret's efforts were unsuccessful, but her formidable character can be seen in defying the king, even if he was her cousin. Sir Walter Mauny was also taking a risk by aiding her illegal travel abroad. Who was Walter Mauny? He would be Margaret's second husband and it's highly likely this was a love match, because of the risks they were happy to take in 1350, plus the fact they married not long after Segrave's death in April 1353 and risked doing so without licence.

Walter Mauny, sometimes known as Manny (c.1310–1372), was a son of a lord in Hainault, an area that now straddles the border of Belgium and France, and was in the service of Willem I, Count of Hainault. Willem I's eldest daughter, Margareta, had originally been the subject of a marriage proposal to the young prince Edward by his father, Edward

II, between 1318 and 1321, but it was her younger sister, Philippa, who married prince Edward in exchange for military assistance after negotiations with Queen Isabella in 1326. They were betrothed by proxy in November 1326 and married in York in January 1328 aged thirteen/fourteen (Queen Philippa's date of birth is not known for sure but considered to be around c.1314) and fifteen respectively. Incidentally, another sister of Philippa, Johanna, had a daughter called Elisabeth who would marry the cousin of Alice of Norfolk and Margaret, John, Earl of Kent, the posthumous son of Edmund of Woodstock.[12]

Walter Mauny was a page in the household of Queen Philippa when she journeyed to England in December 1327, and was a successful soldier who quickly rose in Edward's favour, especially during the Scots wars, amassing lands and wealth. Edward III knighted him in 1331. He also had the patronage of Thomas of Brotherton from 1331, and was one of the distinguished members of Thomas' retinue, along with the likes of Sir Robert Ufford.[13] Margaret therefore would have known Walter Mauny from a young age, just as she did Segrave.

John Segrave died in April 1353 and his sixteen-year-old daughter, Elizabeth, was named as heir, his only surviving son, John, having predeceased him.[14] Margaret married Walter Mauny, without licence (signs of that formidable woman again), shortly after, or at least by, May 1354; on 30 May 1354 Edward III had, in his anger at Margaret, seized all of Segrave's property pertaining to her. In July the same year, Edward III ordered the constable of Somerton Castle in Lincolnshire to take delivery of Margaret and her household, and that Walter 'may stay with her if he so wishes'. She was to stay in the castle, in utmost comfort, although Walter and her household had freedom of movement 'until the king has declared his will to the constable upon the matter, as the king wishes her to stay there for some time at his will'. Although Margaret had her property back at this point, she wasn't officially pardoned by her cousin the king until December 1355, whereby she was pardoned for 'her contempt against the king adjudged upon her in the king's court, in crossing to foreign parts against his prohibition', and to 'Walter and Margaret for intermarrying without the king's licence.'[15]

The chronology and detail of the children born of Margaret from both marriages carries some confusion. Chronicles, peerages and contemporary records didn't necessarily record details of children or family members who had passed away. Margaret's children, discussed below, are the ones with evidence; for example, Margaret Segrave's granddaughter, who gave rise to the Howard dukes of Norfolk today. There are, however, some interesting snippets to the children Margaret probably had but aren't necessarily recorded.

A contemporary source, the register of Corpus Christi College, Cambridge University, was transcribed in 1903 by Mary Bateson. On page fifty-six, covering the years 1357–1358, we find a list of those family members of Margaret who are *vivi* (alive) and those that are *mortui* (dead). *Vivi* are: Master Walter de Manny; Margareta Mareschal, *uxor ejus* (his wife with reference to the Earl Marshalship she inherited from her father); Anna de Manny and Isabella de Manny *filie eorundem* (daughters of the same); and Elisabeth de Mouubrag *filis dicte Margareta* – this is Elizabeth Segrave, daughter of Margaret, who had married John Mowbray, 4th Baron Mowbray (the transcript wrongly says the 3rd baron). *Mortui* are: *Dominus* Thomas de Brotherton *Comes Mareschal;* Alicia *uxor ejus* (Alice Hales, his wife); Edwardus *filius eorundem,* (son of the same); Alicia *filia eorundem,* (daughter of the same, so this is Alice of Norfolk); Johannes de Segrave (John Segrave, Margaret's first husband. Then, interestingly, comes *Johannes et Johannes filii dicti Johannis Segrave,* meaning John and John, sons of said John Segrave; Margareta *filia dicti Johannis Segrave,* (daughter of the said John Segrave); and finally *Walterus* child – Walter's child. By this contemporary source, one can safely assume that Margaret had had four children by Sir John Segrave – John, John, Elizabeth and Margaret. One of the John's would be the son and heir that had died by 1350, possibly by the plague outbreak that likely took Alice's two eldest children. Elizabeth, Lady Mowbray, Margaret and Segrave's only surviving child, will be discussed below. The entry ends thus: '*Et pro omnibus vivis et defunctis pro quibus dictus dominus Walterus et dicta domina Margareta tenentur*' – and for all the living and the dead, for whom the said lord Walter and the said mistress Margaret are bound.[16]

Margaret and Walter Mauny are noted in antiquarian genealogies as also having a son and heir, Thomas Mauny, who died in his youth, predeceasing his father by drowning in a well, aged ten. Thomas was not mentioned by name in the Cambridge Gild Register, but a *Walterus Child* was, and although there appears to be no fourteenth-century contemporary evidence of this young Thomas – the antiquarians do not reference this bit of information – Margaret and Walter had obviously lost a child, so this is possibly him.[17]

The Segrave Children and Grandchildren

Margaret of Norfolk, Lady Segrave and John Segrave's only surviving child was a girl, Elizabeth Segrave (b.1338–d.1366/8), born at Croxton Abbey on 25 October 1338, a couple of months after the death of her grandfather, Thomas, Earl of Norfolk. But was she the firstborn child? Archer, in her 1987 study *The Estates and Finances of Margaret of Brotherton*, notes that 'her son John was her eldest child', and we have seen the Cambridge Gild Register noted that Margaret had two sons named John. Margaret was only around sixteen years old when Elizabeth was born, and her brother John followed two years later in 1340 (d.1353). It is not known when Margaret's other son, also John, was born or when he died, but he was possibly born between Elizabeth and John, or even before Elizabeth – they could even have been twins. The fact he was called John means he was possibly born first, named after his father, died young and the next son was also called John after his brother and their father; after all, in medieval England, the reuse of names of children that had died was common practice.[18]

After the failed negotiations regarding the double betrothal of Edward and Audrey Montagu to John and Blanche Mowbray in 1343, the two Mowbray children went on to marry Elizabeth and John Segrave in March 1349. Elizabeth Segrave married John Mowbray, 4th Baron Mowbray, and became the sole heir of her father, John Segrave, after her brother predeceased their father and proved her age in September 1353 after her father's death in May of the same year. However, Elizabeth and her husband, John Mowbray, inherited just a small amount of the Segrave inheritance as her mother, Margaret, held onto vast amounts when she became a widow.[19]

The chronology of Margaret of Norfolk's Segrave grandchildren, Elizabeth and John Mowbray's children, is confusing and rather convoluted, with dates of birth quite variable, and it appears Elizabeth was facing childbirth more or less every other year from age eighteen or nineteen until her death, aged around thirty, in 1368/9. They had five children altogether, two sons and three daughters, who are listed below in assumed birth order using evidence from genealogist and historians Brad Verity and Douglas Richardson. As with most sources, these dates can be open to interpretation and although the legal age of marriage for females was twelve, there would have likely been occasions where girls were not only betrothed but could be married before the age of seven and would have to give their own consent once maturity was reached.[20]

Eleanor Mowbray was likely born a few years earlier than originally considered, possibly around 1356–57. Her usual given birth date of March 1364 is due to an *inspeximus* confirmation dated 28 April 1369. *Inspeximus* is an examination of earlier charters and/or letters patent and the validity of these earlier agreements has been confirmed. Confirmation was given of an indenture that John Mowbray had 'letters patent … on the Annunciation, 38 Edward III [March 1364], granted for life to his servant John de Disworth for the news which he brought him of the deliverance of his wife, of Eleanor her first daughter, an annuity of 40s out of the manor of Melton Moubray.'[21] It must be noted that this isn't confirmation of Eleanor's birth, just her father's gift to a servant, although if Eleanor was born before 1360, John Mowbray waited quite a while before gifting his servant, for what could be a myriad of reasons. Richardson cites a charter dealing with lands bestowed upon Eleanor and her husband, Lord John Welles, after the death of Welles's father in 1361 but before Mowbray's death in 1368. Therefore, Eleanor had been legally married by 1368 so would have been at least twelve years old, possibly betrothed younger. Her younger sister, Margaret Mowbray, married Reginald de Lucy at Bretby Castle, Derby, according to a marriage licence dated 1 July 1369, making Margaret's birth c.1357.[22]

On 2 April 1369 the *inspeximus* of an indenture that John Mowbray had, in August 1365, 'granted to Joan de Canleye, damsel of his wife, for bringing news of the birth of his eldest son, a rent of 10 marks out the said manor for life'.[23] The eldest son and heir, John, is therefore usually considered to have been born August 1365, but Verity notes that the jurors in his father's Inquisition Post Mortem (IPM) disagree, with the Essex and Sussex IPM's being more specific about his year of birth; most likely John Junior was born by August 1364.[24] He was knighted in April 1377, along with the future Richard II and future Henry IV, and created the 1st Earl of Nottingham in July 1377 during the coronation of Richard II. John Mowbray sadly died young and unmarried in 1383 and was buried at Whitefriars in London.[25]

The next child was a second son, Thomas, born March 1366, whose own IPM gave a very specific date of birth for him: 'He was aged 33 years and 26 weeks on 22 Sept. when he died.'[26] This helps justifying moving John's birth back a year as there is no way Thomas could be born in March 1366 if John had been born in August 1365, especially when women were physically out of bounds to their husbands for four to six weeks, until they were churched, after the birth of a child. Thomas' date of birth is too specific to be ignored and became the Mowbray heir after the premature death of his brother John.

Joan, youngest daughter and final child was born around 1367/8, bearing in mind Elizabeth Segrave died in 1368, most likely in childbirth. Joan had married, by 1382, Sir Thomas Grey (b.c.1359), son of Sir Thomas Grey, the author of the famous *Sacralonica* chronicle. This chronicle, commenced in 1355 whilst Sir Thomas Grey the Elder was a prisoner of the Scots is, in the words of its compiler, 'together with the general information which he has recorded concerning the civil and military transactions of the reigns of Edward II and III, obtained, no doubt, either by his own personal observation, or from the testimony of eye-witnesses, render this history exceedingly valuable.'[27] Thomas

Grey died in December 1400 and Joan had remarried, by 1407, Sir Thomas Tunstall and herself had died by September 1410.[28] Joan and Thomas Grey went on to have four sons and one daughter, some of whom played major political roles in the early 1400s. Their firstborn son and heir, Thomas (1384–1415), was a squire in the household of Henry IV and was married to Alice Neville, the daughter of Ralph Neville, the Earl of Westmorland, in 1398. Around this time, possibly to mark the occasion of the wedding, Sir Thomas and Joan obtained Wark Castle and its manor from Ralph Neville, in exchange for some of their Northumbrian lands. Wark Castle plays a vital role for Edward III with regard to Alice of Norfolk, discussed in a later chapter. Thomas, the son and heir, was executed for treason on 2 August 1415 for his part in a conspiracy to overthrow the new king, Henry V. Joan's second son, John (b. c.1388–1421) fought at Agincourt and was created Count of Tancarville, becoming a military favourite with Henry V. John married a daughter of the lord of Powys but died at the Battle of Bauge in his early thirties. Joan's third son, William (b. c.1390–1436) became Bishop of London in 1426 and then Bishop of Lincoln in 1431. A fourth son, Henry (b. c.1391/95–1454) became a sheriff and member of Parliament in Norfolk, and Joan's only daughter, Maud/Matilda (b. c.1386–after 1454) married Sir Richard Ogle of Northumberland (c.1370–1436) in May 1399 and went on to have three sons and four daughters who all made good marriages.[29]

Elizabeth Segrave and John Mowbray gave rise to the Howard dukes of Norfolk, who still hold the title today with Edward William Fitzalan-Howard currently being the 18th Duke of Norfolk, via their second son, Thomas (b.1366–d. September 1399), whose young daughter, Margaret, married Sir Robert Howard, a Suffolk knight, and whose great-grandmother, Katherine, was the sister of William Ufford, 2nd Earl of Suffolk and Walter Ufford, and therefore sister-in-law of Alice's children, Joan and Elizabeth. It is believed that Thomas was so named after Elizabeth pleaded to St Thomas (just like her great grandmother, Queen Marguerite did) for safety due to her illness either during or after the birth of her son Thomas. Although not stated that she died at this time, Elizabeth was most certainly dead by the time of her husband's Inquisition Post Mortem in early 1369 as she is noted as 'Elizabeth, his late wife'. John Mowbray had died overseas, probably in the summer of 1368.[30] Both Elizabeth and John Mowbray died young.

After the death of their elder son and heir, John, Earl of Nottingham in February 1383 (b. c.August 1364), his younger brother, Thomas Mowbray, became the son and heir and was also elevated to the dukedom of Norfolk in 1397. Although a capable soldier and close ally of the king Richard II, their friendship and his loyalty soon waned; Thomas was implicated in the murder of Thomas of Woodstock, Duke of Gloucester (b.1355–d.1397), youngest son of Edward III, in Calais where Mowbray was governor. Mowbray had also married his second wife without royal licence and early in 1399 was sent into life exile abroad. He was in Venice by February 1399, and his grandmother, Margaret of Norfolk, died in March of the same year. His inheritance from Margaret was seized by Richard II and Thomas Mowbray died later that year, most likely from plague.[31] It was Thomas' second son, John, who became son and heir after his eldest son, also Thomas, was beheaded for treason in 1405. John, 2nd Duke of Norfolk, became the first Mowbray to be reconciled with the Brotherton and Segrave lands in 1413, and after the death of his mother, Elizabeth FitzAlan in 1425, the first Mowbray to reside at Framlingham Castle.[32]

John Segrave, son and heir of Margaret of Norfolk and Sir John Segrave, was born 13 September 1340 at the the Segrave's Bretby Castle in Derbyshire. In May 1347 a mighty marriage betrothal was made between the young John Segrave and Blanche of Lancaster, the younger daughter of King Henry III's great-grandson and one of the most powerful and wealthiest peers of the realm, Henry of Grosmont, 1st Duke of Lancaster (c.1310–d.1361) and his wife, Isabella de Beaumont. Why mighty? Blanche was co-heir with her sister Matilda (also known as Maud) to her father's great estates (and eventual sole heir when her sister died in 1362 with no issue). However, the marriage never took place and Blanche went on to marry John of Gaunt, the third surviving son of Margaret's cousin, King Edward III, becoming the mother and grandmother of King Henry IV and Henry V respectively.[33]

Two years later, in March 1349, young John Segrave married Blanche Mowbray in a joint ceremony with his sister, Elizabeth Segrave, who, as we have seen, married Blanche's brother, John Mowbray, son and heir to John, 3rd Lord Mowbray, and his wife, Joan of Lancaster. Joan was the sister of Henry, 1st Duke of Lancaster, thus John Segrave was now marrying Henry's niece, not his daughter. There was no issue from this marriage as, unfortunately, the young John Segrave had died by his father's death in 1353 and possibly by 1350, most likely caused by the plague outbreak of 1349. As was mentioned in the last chapter on Alice, it was Blanche and John Mowbray who were originally, and unsuccessfully, betrothed to Alice's children, Edward and Audrey Montagu.[34]

The Mauny Children and Grandchildren

Only Anne Mauny survived long enough to have one grandchild. The Cambridge Gild Register shows us that Margaret and Walter Mauny also had a child who died young, and another daughter, Isabel, who was alive at the time of the compilation of the register in 1357/8 but who had died by her father's death in 1372, which correlates with Anne being named as the only heir in her father's Inquisition Post Mortem.[35] Margaret's second surviving daughter and longest-lived child, Anne Mauny, was born in 1355, and in July 1368 she was married to the twenty-one-year-old John Hastings, 2nd Earl of Pembroke (b.1347–d.1375). Even at that young age, John was already a widower, with Anne being his second wife. Aged eleven, John Hastings had firstly been married, in 1359, to the eleven-year-old Margaret of Windsor (b.1346–d.1361), daughter of Edward III, with whom he had grown up and who was a distant cousin of Anne:

To the archbishop of Canterbury. Mandate, on petition of king Edward, to dispense, if the facts be as stated, John de Hastinges,

Earl of Pembroke, and Ann, daughter of Walter de Many (Mauny), knight, damsel, of the dioceses of Canterbury and Cambray, to intermarry, notwithstanding that Ann was related, in the third and fourth degrees of kindred, to the late Margaret, daughter of king Edward, damsel, whom the said earl had married. The said earl and Ann are exhorted, if the dispensation be granted, to give 1000 gold florins towards the repair of the church of the monastery of St. Paul, Rome.[36]

Margaret of Windsor died sometime after October 1361 (another plague victim?), aged approximately fifteen, and they had no issue.[37]

John, 2nd Earl of Pembroke, was the only son of Laurence Hastings, 1st Earl of Pembroke, and his wife, Agnes, daughter of Roger Mortimer, 1st Earl of March, the de facto ruler of Edward III's early reign. John had a strong military career abroad for the king and was back in England in early 1372, when a sixteen-year-old Anne conceived their first and, as it turned out, only child. John was taken captive later that same year during the Battle of La Rochelle in June 1372. The conditions he was kept in are believed to have led to his death on 16 April 1375, just as ransom negotiations were taking place and as he was being moved from Paris to Calais for the journey back to England.[38]

As countess of Pembroke, Anne produced a son and heir, John, 3rd Earl of Pembroke (1373–December 1389), although, as we have seen, he would never know his father. Anne shared the care of her son with her mother, Margaret, Countess of Norfolk (in her own right at this stage) although the marriage of the young John was given to John of Gaunt, a younger son of Edward III and Margaret's cousin. Gaunt arranged the betrothal of his younger daughter, Elizabeth of Lancaster, to the young Earl of Pembroke and they were married at Kenilworth Castle in 1380; John was eight years old compared to Elizabeth's seventeen years. The marriage was annulled in 1386 after Elizabeth of Lancaster became pregnant by John Holland, second son of Margaret and Alice's cousin, Joan of Kent, and they were subsequently married. The thirteen-year-old John, 3rd Earl of Pembroke, was returned to the care of his grandmother, Margaret, as his mother, Anne, had died in April 1384, surviving her husband and leaving her then eleven-year-old son and heir in the wardship of King Richard II, Edward III's grandson.[39] Although he went on to marry a second time, John was tragically killed, aged seventeen, after receiving a mortal groin injury by Sir John St John (also known as Sir John Des) during practice at a Christmas joust held by Richard II at Woodstock in December 1389.[40] The Mauny-Norfolk lineage died with him as he left no issue.

As noted in the previous chapter, Alice of Norfolk's surviving youngest daughter and heir, Joan, Countess of Suffolk, and all five of Joan's children had died by August 1375, bringing all of the Brotherton Norfolk inheritance back together under Margaret. By the time of the death of her grandson, John Hastings, via the Mauny line in 1389, Margaret of Norfolk had outlived all her family bar one – Thomas Mowbray, her Segrave grandson by her daughter Elizabeth – making Margaret one of the wealthiest women in the kingdom. Her wealth had been helped by the fourteenth-century legal practice of allowing freedom of tenant-in-chiefs in disposing of land as they saw fit, including endowing jointure (joint tenancy of lands/rents/properties) to wives. John Segrave took this action by endowing jointure on Margaret for all his property, which had earlier deprived their daughter, Elizabeth Segrave, of inheriting the Segrave property.[41]

In 1371 and 1372 Margaret gave over the administration of her Irish lands and her Chepstow estates respectively to her son-in-law, the earl of Pembroke, husband of her daughter Anne Mauny. Margaret took back control after his death in 1375 and it appears an intelligent and independent Margaret was astute when it came to managing her vast wealth. A study by Dr Rowena Archer in 1987 on Margaret's finances shows a woman with business acumen and effective management skills on estates no matter where they lay geographically. A good example of this is South Wales and the lordship of Chepstow (also known as *Striguil*), which Margaret inherited on the death of her stepmother, Mary, Countess of Norfolk, in 1362. Margaret's accounts show this to be one of her most valuable assets and although administration of such

huge estates must have been difficult, her accounts show her staying at
Chepstow in 1385–86. However, it was also Chepstow that showed a
darker side to Margaret. Sometime between 1387 and 1388 Margaret
petitioned her Chepstow lordship rights over four neighbouring manors
– Magor, Redwick, Porton and Pill. She made a claim for these, stating
that they belonged to the ancient lineage of her father's ancestors and
this included jurisdiction within the court of Chepstow, where she had
been demanding the king's tenants of these manors to appear in her
court. These four manors had been divided away from the Chepstow
lordship when the estate was partitioned between the five daughters of
William Marshall between 1245 and 1250.[42]

An inquisition in August 1388 sees Margaret accused of being unjust
and using usurpation against the king's tenants-in-chief of the same four
manors. One of those named is Sir Hugh Durbergh, who was noted as
the tenant-in-chief, and who, earlier in the year, on 19 February 1388,
was granted a licence to grant his manor of Magor to a James Durbergh,
his wife, Alice, and heirs of their body. This clearly shows the lordship
of Chepstow did not extend to Magor (although today classed as being
in Monmouthsire and only a short drive from Chepstow, Magor was
under the county of Gloucester in 1388).[43]

In the same 1388 inquisition in August, Margaret was also accused of
punishment and oppression of the king's tenants in the form of ransoms
and fines, and had been doing this for the past ten years. However, on
21 October 1388, at the king's court in Magor, things had taken a step
further. Margaret's parker, ranger and forester, along with over twenty
named bailiffs and tenants of Margaret, armed with 'hauberks, breast-
plates, swords, bucklers, cudgels, bows, arrows and other arms' assaulted
and killed tenants of Magor after 'crossing boundaries'. Any settlement
is unknown, but Margaret was still claiming jurisdiction of Chepstow
over the men of Magor, Redwick, Porton and Pill in 1390.[44]

Whilst Margaret may have wanted these manors back under
the ancestral lineage of Chepstow, it is also worth considering how
financially viable the area was due to the immediate geography of
the Severn Estuary, as well as the surrounding farmland. The estuary

was a major trade artery in medieval times and had been since early settlements, as evidenced in the remains of Iron Age hillforts along the estuary today. Chepstow had a thriving and busy port with direct access and trade links to the bigger Bristol port. The area was a wealthy haven for fishing, and Margaret had the world-famous Chepstow salmon, as well as Chepstow lampreys, transported to Framlingham Castle. Sitting at the confluence of the River Wye and the Bristol Channel, the salmon had a unique taste and texture, so much so that it even had its own poem by the 1700s.[45] Since the Roman era, Magor had been home to an ancient harbour called *Abergwaitha*, although this began to fall out of favour during the fourteenth century due to coastal erosion. The remains of a thirteenth-century trading boat were found nearby in 1994, showing a cargo of iron ore, which had been mined in the area since pre-Roman times. The area was also home to Lower Grange, a farmstead under the control of Tintern Abbey and Goldcliff Priory, one of the three wealthiest priories of Wales at this time.[46]

Margaret was respected deeply by others of the nobility. The power magnates of the day, such as the Lancasters, Beauchamps and the Arundels, appeared to hold Margaret in high regard and affection. During her time as Lady Segrave, she had given Thomas Beauchamp, Earl of Warwick, a piece of the 'true cross' and this was remembered in his will.[47] Margaret is also remembered in the Earl of Arundel's will in 1392 by being bequeathed a gold cross, and her cousin, John of Gaunt, Duke of Lancaster, offered her New Year presents and often sought alliances with her.[48] These alliances worked for Margaret (and we have seen that her sharp brain, business acumen and self-esteem was in no short supply), and it is more than likely she held the reins of power in East Anglia, which was useful for the Duke of Lancaster. John of Gaunt's son, Henry Bolingbroke (later Henry IV) sent his own son, John, Duke of Bedford, to be educated at Framlingham Castle, Norfolk, under Margaret's care. This is where Margaret herself had most likely been born, and she had also set up Framlingham as her own home in widowhood in 1382.[49]

As Margaret already held the earldom of Norfolk as her father's only surviving heir, she was elevated to Duchess of Norfolk in her own right by her first cousin-twice-removed King Richard II when her only surviving grandchild, Thomas Mowbray, was created Duke of Norfolk in September 1397. When she died on 24 March 1399 her grandson, Thomas Mowbray, should have inherited her vast wealth and estates. He was, however, an exile in Venice at the time of Margaret's death and his letters patent, securing any inheritances that may come to him during his exile, were revoked by Richard II. Thomas died just seven months after his grandmother after contracting plague. It was Thomas' daughter, Margaret Mowbray, Margaret's great-granddaughter, who gave rise to the dukes of Norfolk today.[50]

Margaret had died at Framlingham and chose to be buried at the wealthy and grandiose priory of the Greyfriars in London. The original monastery had consisted of just two buildings on a plot bought for the men of the Franciscan Order by a wealthy London merchant, John Iwyn, in the summer of 1225. At that time it was an unsavoury, no-go area after dark but the populace were precisely the people who needed such hospitality and support. By 1243 the numbers had grown from just four clerks and five lay brothers to eighty friars and was considerably extended over the next fifteen years.[51] Margaret's paternal grandmother, Queen Marguerite, became enamoured of Greyfriars and had generously endowed land and money for building works in 1301–02. In 1352–53 Edward II's wife and Marguerite's niece, Queen Isabella, also generously endowed the church choir, and in 1380 Margaret of Norfolk spent 350 marks on new timber to replace the choir stalls. All three of these ladies were buried in the choir of Greyfriars, Margaret of Norfolk in the central area.[52] By 1306 Greyfriars had a sizeable and lavish frontage along Newgate Street of which little remains today. Greyfriars fell victim to the Dissolution in 1538 with the loss of many tombs, and the original buildings were reused, the most famous one being Christ's Hospital (a school founded in 1553 by Edward VI). The buildings were ruined in the Great Fire of London in 1666, but the church was rebuilt by Wren, who also rebuilt the nearby St Paul's. Unfortunately, the church was lost in the Blitz in 1940 and what remains today is a hollowed-out interior which serves as a garden to escape the hubbub of London. It is hardly recognisable as what was once, allegedly, the second largest medieval church in London and a seat of learning from its inception in 1225 to the Dissolution. At the time of Queen Marguerite's endowment, the famous philosopher and theologian William of Ockham was teaching there before he left for Oxford.

Margaret was buried with neither of her two husbands. John Segrave chose to be buried with other members of the Segrave family, at Chacombe Priory in Northamptonshire, also spelt Chaucombe and Chalcombe. The priory had a long history with the Segraves and in 1326 it was confirmed that its patron, Stephen Segrave, and his heirs were free to choose 'a man at the gate, at the costs of the house, to guard the goods'.[53]

Walter Mauny requested to be buried in the high altar at the London Charterhouse, a Carthusian monastery that he had founded in 1371, although he had initiated the foundation nearly twenty years previously.[54] In the summer of 1348 the plague had come to southern England and burial ground space for plague victims was fast running out. St Bartholomew's hospital for the sick and poor in Smithfield, Middlesex – which had been founded in 1163 and is now a large teaching hospital known as St Bart's in the City of London – came to an agreement to rent out some of its land known as Spital Croft (*spital* is a derivation of the word hospital) with Walter Mauny who, as an act of piety and charity, rented the thirteen acres of land as a plague burial pit on condition that when he provided a property of equal value then he could have the land. On 25 March 1349 the burial land was dedicated by the Bishop of London, Ralph Stratford, and a few years later Mauny was in discussions with Michael Northburgh, Bishop of London 1355–61, regarding the founding of a Carthusian monastery on the site. Discussions and arrangements including building works with the Carthusian Monks took until 1371 for an agreement and the Charterhouse became richly endowed very quickly. However, these initial endowments, such as a gift of £2000 by Northburgh, Bishop of London, articles of plate (such as bowls and goblets) from the church, various manors owned by Mauny, as well as a debt of £4000 owed by Edward III and the Black Prince to Mauny that he asked to go to his new foundation, soon proved unsustainable; the lands were stolen and flooded and the royal debt never honoured. Thereafter, a steady stream of income was made by wills from wealthy donors and Londoners, including property, estates and money.[55] A licence was granted in February 1371: 'Licence for Walter, lord of Mauny, knight, to found a house of Westminster monks of the Carthusian order, to wit, a prior and certain monks, to be called "the Salutation of the Mother of God in honour of God and the Blessed Virgin Mary", on his own soil in a place without the bar of Westsmethefeld, London, called "la Newecherche Hawe", not held in chief, and to endow it with certain lands.'[56] Mauny died at Margaret's manor of Great Chesterford in Essex in January 1372, less than a year after his new foundation, and so popular was he that his funeral was attended by Edward III and all of his sons bar the Black Prince who was ill. Like many medieval tombs, Mauny's was thought lost after Henry VIII's Reformation, but it was rediscovered after the Second World War. Sir Walter Mauny's remains were excavated and reburied in Chapel Court, marked near the entrance of today's Charterhouse Museum.[57]

Chapter 3

Thomas of Brotherton, Earl of Norfolk

Thomas Brodirton Erle of Norfolke, cam doun into Norfolke, and ther he wedded a Knygthis Doughter, fast be Bungey, and thei hadden togedir ii Dowters, of the which, oon hight Margeret, and the toder hight Alice.
                                                                        Blomefield, 1806

Edward I was born at Westminster Palace in June 1239, the first child and son to King Henry III of England (b.1207–d.1272) and his queen consort, Eleanor of Provence (b. c.1223–d.1291). Edward was an unusual name for a royal prince at this time, being of Anglo-Saxon origin, and none had been thus named since the Norman Conquest in 1066. However, growing up, Henry III had developed a devotion and allegiance to Edward the Confessor, making Westminster his base, and it is likely that the birth of first child at Westminster, built by Edward the Confessor, is no coincidence.[1]

In 1254, to settle a political fracas over Gascony, Henry III of England and Alfonso X of Castile, agreed to the marriage alliance of the heir to the throne of England, the fifteen-year-old Lord Edward, to the thirteen-year-old Eleanor of Castile, half-sister to king Alfonso X, and they were married in Castile on 1 November 1254.[2] King Henry III died in August or September 1272 while Edward was on Crusade, and although Edward was declared king at this time, England was being managed successfully by a royal council. It appears Edward did not therefore hurry back, returning to England on 2 August 1274, and finally crowned king on 19 August 1274. It was, however, still a lavish affair. Preparing Westminster for the coronation – including new thrones, temporary buildings and new kitchens – cost in the region of £1100, approximately £900,000 today.[3]

It is well known of the success of the marriage between Edward I and Eleanor of Castile, proving to be both fruitful and happy, rather unusual for the era and much lauded by historians. Eleanor died on 28 November 1290, in the village of Harby in Nottinghamshire, possibly from malaria that she had contracted during their last visit to Gascony in 1287, and Edward's grief was palpable. He spent a few days mourning in Harby then personally escorted her funeral cortege over 200 miles to Westminster, famously erecting magnificent stone cross monuments in each area where Eleanor's body rested overnight. These became known as the Eleanor Crosses and there were twelve overall, most of which were destroyed in the English Civil War by Cromwell's forces, although the remains of two and one that is renovated still stand today. The first was erected at Lincoln, their first stop, where Eleanor's body was embalmed and her viscera buried in a fine tomb at Lincoln Cathedral. A fragment of Eleanor's carved stone dress is all that remains of the original cross, now situated outside Lincoln Castle. Next was Grantham where it is thought any surviving stones from the Eleanor Cross were used in the rebuilding of a market cross. Then came Stamford where only the steps of the original cross were evident in 1745 and have since been replaced with a modern cross in honour of the original. The best surviving cross, though much renovated, is at Geddington, the next stop after Stamford, with another much-renovated cross at the next stop, Hardingstone. At Stony Stratford a high street plaque honours the lost cross, then Woburn where no trace of it exists. Next is the Dunstable cross, which was there in the sixteenth century but is now marked by a plaque, and at the next stop in St Albans, despite some record of the stone remains in 1703, there is no trace today. Waltham Abbey had the stone cross restored at the next stop in Cheapside, where a modern stone cross commemorates the original that was destroyed by Cromwell's troops in 1643. At the small village of Charing a stone cross was erected at the site of a road junction, now the site of Trafalgar Square. This was the most elaborate and expensive, destroyed in 1647 by those pesky Cromwellian troops again, then rebuilt in Victorian times to elaborate the entrance of the new Charing Cross Railway. It was here, at her request, that Eleanor's heart was buried, in the Dominican abbey of the Blackfriars, alongside that of her son, Alphonso, who died as a child. The abbey was unfortunately destroyed in Henry VIII's Dissolution of the Monasteries. Eleanor's final resting place in December 1290 was at Westminster Abbey, and though her triple burial and monumental crosses set a precedent for an English queen, it was also an obvious sign of Edward's devotion to his wife, who was, at least in the beginning, widely disliked by the English during her lifetime.[4] On her deathbed she asked Edward I to restore any lands and manors that she had unjustly taken from others, which he did. It also came to light how shameful Eleanor had been in her estate managements, 'high-handed and ruthless'. Edward I would not remarry for another nine years, and this was, again, politically motivated. It is this second marriage that gave rise to the Norfolk Plantagenets.[5]

It is likely that Edward's second marriage wasn't expected to be such a close companionship as he had enjoyed with Eleanor. At Canterbury on 10 September 1299, nine years after the death of his beloved Eleanor, sixty-year-old Edward I married the twenty-year-old Marguerite of France (b. c.1279–d. 4 February 1318), from the French royal house of Capet, the youngest child of King Phillippe III of France and his second wife, Marie de Brabant. Although Marguerite wore a crown at her wedding, she was never crowned queen. She was attractive, with the contemporary English chronicler Peter Langtoft noting her as 'good without lack',[6] and it is well known that the twenty-year-old forged good relationships with her stepchildren, who were then aged between fifteen (Prince Edward) and twenty-seven (Joanna) and therefore close in age to Marguerite. A good friendship was struck particularly with the youngest daughter of Edward and Eleanor, Elizabeth of Rhuddlan (b.1282–d.1316). Married aged fourteen to the twelve-year-old Count of Holland, Johan I, and widowed aged seventeen, Elizabeth returned to England in August 1300 and made her way to Cawood Castle where she would meet her baby half-brother, Thomas of Brotherton. Elizabeth spent a lot of time with Marguerite thereafter, even being involved with intercessions together, including a pardon for murder.[7] Elizabeth's sister, Mary of Woodstock (b.1279–d. c.1332), a nun of Amesbury Priory, was also one of the more frequent visitors to the household of her half-siblings, visiting eleven times between June and October 1305, and staying at least five days each visit.[8] Although this may seem unusual for a nun, Mary was no ordinary nun; she was financially supported by her father, Edward I, and was often away at court and family gatherings for prolonged periods of time.[9] Her extraordinary position will be discussed in a later chapter. Marguerite's niece, Isabella, would go onto to marry Edward I's son by Eleanor, the future Edward II, and Marguerite would also go on to be present at the birth of the future Edward III. Edward I did indeed go on to have a close and solid relationship with his much younger second wife.[10]

Marguerite become pregnant with her first child almost immediately after her wedding to Edward I. Thomas of Brotherton was born on 1 June 1300 and his birth is much written about. Originally, plans were made for Thomas' birth at the Archbishop of Canterbury's Cawood Castle in North Yorkshire, an archiepiscopal residence up until the English Civil War of 1642–1651 when it was then abandoned. Edward I had made Cawood his northern base whilst dealing with the Scottish wars.[11] Marguerite's household accounts show that preparations for the birth, such as food, cloth and other materials, were transported from St Albans to Cawood under the supervision of John of Montabisca, valet of the queen's wardrobe, whilst repairs to Cawood were supervised by a clerk, John of Brentingham, from the Treasurer of the Exchequer. All of this appears to have been successfully – if somewhat hastily – transferred to the village of Brotherton after Marguerite, stopping at the small village in North Yorkshire on 31 May 1300, gave birth to Thomas prematurely the following day, 1 June.[12]

The fact that Marguerite had all the birthing preparation done for Cawood Castle and Thomas was born en route shows she wasn't expecting the birth quite so soon. Some sources state that Marguerite, an experienced horsewoman, enjoyed riding to hounds and was out on a hunt, an activity she was known to enjoy, when she unexpectedly went into labour.[13] However, Marguerite's household roll shows that by the 29 May 1300 she had either fallen behind her schedule or for the last six weeks before Thomas' birth she may have been suffering an illness, or at least feeling unwell, as she was riding in a type of small chariot as well as a litter, for which pillows and a bed were provided for.[14] Contemporary English chroniclers of the day wrote how Marguerite, due to having a difficult labour, invoked the assistance of St Thomas Becket of Canterbury for the safe delivery of the child (and for whom the baby boy was likely named).[15] Also, how the king, when told of the news of the safe delivery of another, much needed son, 'prepares quickly to visit the lady, like a falcon to the wind'.[16] Langtoft also notes how the queen was staying at Brotherton on the Wharf, a village on the river Aire, which is a clue that she must have been in a manor house befitting her station (today it's an eighteenth-century manor house with earlier foundations near the river Aire, possibly on the site of Thomas' birth). Writing in 1941, the journalist Arthur Mee stated that 'the house where he [Thomas of Brotherton] was born has gone but the old manor house built on its site still survives in farm buildings'.[17] Nonetheless, King Edward I had his heir and spare.

The chronicler Rishanger also wrote how the baby Thomas rejected his first wet nurse, becoming unwell, due to the fact she was French, but rallied well when replaced with an English wet nurse.[18] Propaganda perhaps, chronicler's bias possibly, but there may be a grain of truth in the statement, not for the reason of ethnicity but that of illness that seemed to be encompassing the queen's retinue at this time. One of Thomas' nurses named Joan had died suddenly, most likely around November 1300, with Marguerite donating a monetary gift in January 1301 for the funeral. Also in November 1300, Marguerite's maid, Agnes, required the attention of the queen's physician due to illness. In a postscript to her *Welcome, Royal Babe!* study, Staniland notes the possibility that Thomas' wet nurse may have been given medication due to being unwell and this medication would have transferred via the breast milk to the baby Thomas. We have already seen how toxic some medieval medicines could be, so this is a considered possibility.[19]

Merely a year later, at Woodstock Palace, Oxfordshire, Thomas was joined by a baby brother, Edmund of Woodstock (b. 5 August 1301–d. 19

March 1330). A baby sister, Eleanor of England, possibly named after Edward I's first wife although more than likely his mother, Eleanor of Provence (1223–1291), was born in May 1306 in Winchester and was betrothed, aged just a few days old, to the son and heir of the count of Burgundy. Eleanor of England died aged just five years at Amesbury priory in 1311, and was buried at Beaulieu Abbey, a Cistercian abbey founded by King John.[20]

Thomas was assigned his own household before he was a year old, at least by 6 January 1301, and was soon followed into his household by his younger brother, Edmund, later in the year. The king had ordered twenty tuns of wine for Thomas' household, various ornaments and a chaplain had been assigned for Thomas's own chapel. The household was extravagant, nothing short of what was expected as sons of a king. They had their own departments such as stables, kitchens and wardrobes organised by a hierarchy of officials such as the king's own household would be. They had their own Keeper of the Wardrobe (financial matters), a Steward of the Household, knights, wet-nurses, rockers, stable hands and serving boys. During the years 1305–1306, the annual expenditure of the household was in the region of £1300, approximately £750,000 in today's money.[21]

In June 1307 Edward I, who had been ill for a while, rose from his sickbed in Carlisle to advance on the Scots. The chronicler, Walter of Guisborough, stated that the king was suffering from dysentery, an infectious inflammation of the colon that often proved fatal in the time before hygiene and sanitation was fully understood. On 6 July 1307, whilst en route to suppress the Scots, Edward I had to stop at Burgh on Sands due to his illness, where, aged sixty-eight, he died the next day.[22] Edward I's only surviving son from his first marriage, and Thomas' half-brother, now became King Edward II. At seven years old, Thomas of Brotherton found himself only second in importance in the realm as he became heir presumptive, and remained so for the next five years until November 1312 when Edward II's wife, Isabella, niece of dowager Queen Marguerite, gave birth to their firstborn child and son, the future Edward III.[23]

Five years after the death of their father Edward I, in December 1312, Edward II granted his twelve-year-old half-brother, Thomas, the earldom of Norfolk.[24] The earldom had been earmarked for Thomas by their father previously as part of the marriage treaty with Marguerite; the treaty had stated any sons of Marguerite and Edward would be provided with lands valued at 10,000 marks a year (approximately £4.5mn today). In 1306 Roger Bigod, the previous earl of Norfolk, had died without issue and the earldom, plus all that it entailed, including the office of Marshal of England, passed to the Crown after an agreement between Edward I and Roger Bigod in 1302. Although Thomas came into the vacated Bigod earldom, lands and properties in 1312, there is evidence that Thomas held Bungay Castle and manor, Alice's future home, before this date. In July 1310 Edward II granted his younger half-brothers, Thomas and Edmund, their sustenance 'of all the castles, towns, manors and tenements in the king's hands late of Roger le Bygod, sometime earl of Norfolk and marshal of England', and granted John de Thorpe the keeper of said properties and the boys wardrobe accounts.[25] The Suffolk clergyman and historian Alfred Suckling (1796–1856) quotes an ancient charter dated 3 March 1310 from Edward II to the 'earls, barons, knights and others' prohibiting a tournament that was to be held at Bungay (Edward began to prohibit tournaments starting in January 1310 when he similarly prohibited a tournament at Newmarket as at this time, it was believed that tournaments were disguising meetings of the nobility to plot the downfall of the much-hated Piers Gaveston, Edward II's favourite and discussed later in the book).[26] Although Brotherton isn't named, nor is anyone, Bungay would have been one of his due inheritances and both Thomas and his brother would have had a passion for jousting, as seen in their request to the king in 1323 for a tournament in Northampton that Edward II granted, although he subsequently changed his mind.[27]

Thomas of Brotherton was now the wealthy Earl of Norfolk and an extremely important pawn in the marriage stakes, as well as a major player on the political stage. Or so it should have been.[28]

As it turned out, by 1320 both Thomas and his younger brother, Edmund, were still not betrothed or in agreement with anyone, let alone married. Unusual for such high-ranking royals in medieval times, and, as we have seen, exceptional in the sense that neither were yet wed to strengthen their power and the royal purse via a wealthy heiress. Edward II had started negotiations with James II of Aragon regarding the possible marriages of two of James' daughters to Thomas and his own son, the prince Edward (future Edward III). However, for whatever reasons, these negotiations became protracted over the course of 1320–1321 and James II's daughter, Maria (b.1299), a young widow who was proposed for Thomas, had decided instead to take the veil by August 1321.[29]

It turns out that August 1321 was a busy time for the Earl of Norfolk. Not only were relations strained between him and his half-brother, King Edward II, Thomas was also by this time under excommunication for violence. In a letter dated 3 August 1321, the Bishop of Winchester wrote to the Bishop of Salisbury to absolve Thomas of his excommunication for assaulting the bishop's clerk, although no date is mentioned for the affray.[30] To top all that, Thomas married around this time – and seemingly of his own volition – a local Norfolk girl, Alice Hales, the daughter of the local Norfolk coroner, Sir Roger Hales, who held a knight's fee of Thomas, a feudal agreement whereby land was supplied to support a knight and his livelihood in return for military service, and whose son, Alice's brother, John Hales, became a ward of Thomas after Sir Roger's death in 1313. Therefore, Thomas is very likely to have known Alice Hales, born sometime after November 1303, since they were children as the Hales family seat of Loddon Hall was near Bungay Castle.[31]

The marriage of Thomas, Earl of Norfolk, and Alice Hales is very surprising for such a high-ranking member of the nobility. Alice was far beneath Thomas socially, she brought no land, property or any dower to the marriage, and she belonged to a rather obscure lineage, belonging to the social class that would become known as the gentry. Although Alice may have been far below him socially, the union could also be viewed as Thomas strengthening his localised affinity, which in essence was a visible way of showing his status, wealth and provisioning him with a dedicated wartime force, if needed. A magnate's affinity, especially in the fourteenth century, would have consisted of not just household members such as servants and estate officials but also knights, men at arms and tenurial links. Estate officials could be administrators and councillors whilst a wider affinity would consist of other magnates or retainers that were not necessarily in the continuous employ of their lord, or those that could be called upon to assist with localised issues. The Hales family would fall into this category.[32]

The Hales family, however, were rather notorious across East Anglia, and many of Alice Hales' kinsmen appeared to be typical of the criminal faction that received pardons for their military assistance despite their crimes. Alice's own father was himself a victim; Sir Roger Hales was assaulted in early 1303 whilst performing his duties as coroner in Norfolk, when he was attacked by locals who questioned his jurisdiction. In November 1303 we have a pardon for 'Robert de Hales, son of Roger de Hales, of Denston [Suffolk] for robberies and breaking the prison of Stafford.'[33] This must have been one of Alice Hales' brothers. A few years later, in June 1346, we see a pardon at the request of Robert Ufford, Earl of Suffolk, to 'Roger son of John de Hales, "chevalier", of the king's suit for the rape of Alice, daughter of William de Layton, whereof he is appealed and of any consequent outlawry.' John Hales had previously left for Gascony in April 1330 with Thomas of Brotherton straight after the judicial murder of Thomas' brother, the Earl of Kent.[34] John Hales was knighted in 1337, the steward of Thomas Brotherton's household at that time, when Edward Montagu had also been knighted, and at the Battle of Crécy Sir John Hales served in the retinue of Robert Ufford. It is likely that Roger Hales, John's son and therefore Alice Hales' nephew, was in the same retinue. A month later the same Roger was pardoned for 'having ravished and deflowered Alice, his own daughter, whereof she died', as well as assaulting the wife (another Alice) and son, Walter, of Robert Hales (possibly a brother but little is known of the wider family) and entering the house of Walter Red of Hales and assaulting him. 'The king of special grace has pardoned the said Roger the suit of his peace which pertains to him for the rape, felony and trespasses aforesaid.'[35] Another member of the family, William Hales, was a clerk of the church, and in March 1346 was instituted to the rectory of Tunstall, Suffolk by his patron, Edward Montagu, although as we have seen, resigned this position in 1352.[36]

There appears to be no records surviving of the marriage of Thomas and Alice Hales in chronicles, no celebrations or gifts in Edward II's accounts, nor any reprimand, punishment or fine for marrying against the king's wishes. As Thomas had come of age on 1 June 1321, and knew his betrothed Aragon princess had taken the veil in August 1321, it is probable that the marriage occurred at or between these dates, although no actual marriage date appears to be recorded anywhere. Alice Hales may have already been pregnant by August 1321, as they went onto have a son, Edward, who was of marriageable age by 1329.[37]

Whatever the reason for the marriage, be it true love, lust, or to expand his affinity in his East Anglian domains, Alice Hales was now Countess of Norfolk, and if she wasn't already, quickly became pregnant, producing three children over the next four years: a son, Edward, born c.1323, and two daughters, Margaret, born c.1322, and Alice in early 1324.[38] It is not known with any certainty if the only son and heir, Edward of Norfolk, or his sister Margaret was born first, although Edward was married in the summer of 1329 to Beatrice, the younger daughter of the Earl of March, Roger Mortimer, in a double wedding at which Beatrice's sister, Agnes Mortimer, was married to the Earl of Pembroke. This date is sometimes noted as in May 1328, but as the historian Dr Mortimer points out, Roger Mortimer would have to be an earl himself before marrying his two daughters to such esteemed members of the nobility; Roger Mortimer created himself Earl of March in October 1328, his greed hurtling him towards his future downfall in 1330.[39]

Edward of Norfolk must have been at least seven years old, the age of reason for marriage betrothals in the fourteenth century, making his birth year 1322, which is generally considered to be the year of Margaret of Norfolk's birth. Margaret herself gave birth in 1338, and she is usually considered to be sixteen years old at this time, but she could have been a year younger, making her birth year 1323; Margaret is referred to as the eldest daughter in official records. Alice Hales may have already been pregnant when she married Thomas of Brotherton in the summer of 1321, or Edward and Margaret could have been twins, but, sadly, Edward of Norfolk had died sometime before December 1334; at this time in the records, Beatrice is recorded as the wife of Thomas Braose.[40]

Of course, the marriage of Thomas, Earl of Norfolk, and Alice Hales of the gentry class could have been a love match. In 1801 the antiquarian Sir William Betham (1779–1853) noted that Alice Hales 'was so beautiful, as to captivate Thomas de Brotherton, earl of Norfolk.' Unfortunately, he gives no source for his information but as the historian Kathryn Warner states, Alice Hales could have easily been available a mistress, yet Alison Marshall's 2006 study on Thomas proposes he married to build his local affinity and expand his own powerbase across his East Anglian estates where he had most impact.[41] The last mention of Alice Hales, Countess of Norfolk, in official records was on 8 May 1326: 'Grant, at the request of Thomas, Earl of Norfolk and marshal of England, the king's brother, and of Alice, his wife, to Joan Jermye, sister of the said countess, of the marriage of John son and heir of John Lovel, tenant in chief, the king's ward.'[42]

Alice Hales had died by October 1330,[43] aged only in her mid-to-late twenties, so quite possibly during childbirth. Alice of Norfolk was very young when her mother died and would have known her stepmother, Mary Braose, more than she did her own mother.

Before March 1336 Thomas of Brotherton was married for a second time, again far below his social status, to Mary Braose (b. before March 1336–d. 11 June 1362), the widow of Sir Ralph de Cobham (d.1326). Mary was the younger daughter of Sir Peter (Piers) Braose of Tetbury, in Gloucestershire, a cadet branch of the baronial Braose family, also known as Brewes. Thomas of Brotherton would have been more than familiar with this branch of the Braose family. Mary's older brother, Thomas Braose, only a month or so younger than Thomas, inherited his father's baronetcy in 1311/12 and was a household knight of Edward

III, being summoned to military service in 1335 and 1342. The nobility and ruling families certainly kept things involved, if a tad convoluted – it was the son of Beatrice and Thomas Braose, John Braose, who was married to Elizabeth Montagu, the second eldest but first surviving daughter of Thomas' daughter Alice and Edward Montagu.[44] This will be discussed in a later chapter. Thomas Braose went onto marry Beatrice Mortimer, the young widow of Edward of Norfolk, sometime before September 1337, therefore enjoying the wealthy dower estate of Bosham that had been endowed to Edward of Norfolk and Beatrice by Thomas of Brotherton at their wedding in 1329.[45]

Thomas of Brotherton hasn't had a positive narrative by various historians over the years, coming across as overlooked and dull despite being a member of one of the older aristocratic families that managed to survive the turmoil of Edward II's reign, Isabella and Roger's regime, and Edward III's reign, which saw the advent of 'new men' of Edward's circle breathe new life and blood into the nobility. Was he self-absorbed, looking after his own interests or quick-witted enough to tread a fine line of politics that saw his brother Edmund, the Earl of Kent, executed? After all, Thomas did appear to act unexpectedly on occasion, such as seeming to desert the well-being of his brother's young family and heavily pregnant sister-in-law who gave birth shortly after Edmund's execution.

Edmund of Woodstock (August 1301–March 1330) who had been created the Earl of Kent in July 1321 by his half-brother, King Edward II, had married Margaret Wake (b. late 1290s-d. 29 September 1349] in December 1325.[46] Margaret was the widow of John Comyn, who was killed at the Battle of Bannockburn in 1314, and their only son died in infancy. Margaret and Edmund went onto have four children over the next four and a half years, but Edmund would never know his youngest son, who was born posthumously in April 1330, a month after his father had been executed by Roger Mortimer, 1st Earl of March, for allegedly attempting to free his half-brother, Edward II, when rumours abound that he was still alive after his forced abdication by Mortimer and Queen Isabella in January 1327. Margaret's brother, Thomas, Lord Wake, was also implicated and fled abroad. So, when Edmund was executed on 19 March 1330 Margaret was alone, family wise. Mortimer had ordered herself and the children to be taken to Salisbury Castle under arrest, but due to her advanced pregnancy they remained at the Kent family seat of Arundel Castle, where John was subsequently born on 7 April 1330. Thomas of Brotherton had left for Gascony a couple of weeks later, as we saw previously, with his brother-in-law, John Hales.[47] This whole affair will be looked at in a later chapter.

Was Thomas simply distancing himself to save his own life and that of his own family? Did Thomas of Brotherton make bad decisions, such as his choice of wife, or did he marry for love and protocol be damned? The chronicler Jean Froissart (b.c.1337–c.1404) wrote of Thomas as having 'a very wild and fierce temperament,' and his brother Edmund as 'a noble, mild and benevolent man, beloved of the people'.[48] However, in 1328 both Thomas and Edmund had plundered and laid to waste anything and everything they could grasp from the lands of the former favourite of Edward II, Hugh Despenser the Younger, to such a degree that their men earned royal pardons for their behaviour.[49] Froissart's main source of information was the chronicler Jean le Bel (b.c.1290–d.1370) who had been a direct contemporary of Thomas and would most likely have known both him and his brother Edmund. Interestingly, Edmund's untimely death did not necessarily lead to great mourning as he was also remembered for his plundering of the countryside and 'political waverings'.[50] Thomas more than likely had the infamous Plantagenet temper and we have seen that he was excommunicated for assaulting a bishop's clerk. Thomas also appeared not to be a favourite of his nephew Edward III for what could be a myriad of reasons. In October 1331 Edward III ordered Thomas to take back his lands in Ireland from rebels after complaints from the people about the 'wasted lands'. Edward stated that if Thomas did not sort the rebels, and he, the king, had to sort the problem himself, Thomas would forfeit said lands to the Crown.[51]

Thomas of Brotherton begins to fall off the historical and political radar after 1333. Then, in March 1337, Edward III summoned Thomas to court due to complaints regarding his household and his servants. This particular Parliament of March 1337 was a busy one and not a good one for Thomas who was summoned to answer charges of a disorderly household, such as, 'with the assent of the earl who has been summoned before the king and council on account of complaints of oppressions of the people of those parts where the household stayed due to lack of discreet rule and good array thereof and has submitted himself entirely to their disposal.' Included in this summons was a mandate to Sir Ralph Bocking, steward of Thomas' lands, that only those people named on the roll accompanying the summons were to stay within the household. Edward III had appointed the royal servant and local landowner Sir Constance Mortimer to oversee the task and make any changes he deemed fit.[52] Two months later, on 25 May 1337, Edward III removed the office of the Marshalsea from Thomas; this was a high status role whereby an ambulatory court would be held by the king's household steward and knight marshal to oversee jurisdiction between the king and his domestic servants, including breaches of the king's peace within twelve miles of the king's presence (hence ambulatory). However, it must have been returned to him at some point as at his death he was officially referred to as Earl of Norfolk and Marshal of England in the records.[53]

By December 1337 Thomas was in Scotland in the king's service but may have known at this time that he was unwell as only a couple of weeks later, in January 1338, he was back home in England 'where he would be staying'.[54] In the first few months of 1338 an unusually high number of individuals sought confirmation from the king regarding grants that Thomas had made to them. Then in May 1338 Thomas used jointure to secure his most valuable assets, Framlingham and Walton in Suffolk, for his second wife, Mary, and again in June 1338 for the castle and town of Chepstow with reversion to his heirs.[55] By this time, Thomas had had no issue with Mary, but of his three children by Alice Hales, his son and heir, Edward, had predeceased him, Alice was married to Edward Montagu, and Margaret was Lady Segrave, pregnant with her first child. On 4 August 1338 Thomas was at Framlingham when he made his will and died around 25 August 1338. His widow, Mary, Countess of Norfolk, died in 1362 after efficiently managing the Brotherton estates for her stepdaughter Margaret to step into her inheritance as countess of Norfolk *suo jure*.[56]

For an earl of Norfolk, son, brother and uncle to three successive kings, Thomas of Brotherton doesn't exactly leap off the pages of history or illuminate antiquarian tomes. Despite the chronicle *Vita Edwardi Secundi* (known as simply *Vita*) stating that both Thomas and Edmund were active soldiers despite their ages of only twenty-one and twenty respectively – '*Conuenerunt autem in auxilium domini regis duo fratres sui, uidelicet Thomas comes Marescallus et Edmundus comes Cancie, pro etate strenui.*'[57] – further opinion of Thomas has mostly been one of dullness, accusing him of not being particularly bright or astute when dealing with other magnates in the business of land transactions and marriage arrangements (regarding both of his children and of himself). His choice of marriages is questionable and could be seen as wasted opportunities that highlight his lack of astuteness. The genealogist Brad Verity, being of the opinion Thomas was a 'political non-entity' puts forward an idea that his difficult birth may have had an impact on his cognitive ability, and although this will never be known for sure, it is a possibility that his premature, traumatic birth did indeed cause some cognitive issues, usually caused by hypoxia, for example.[58] However, it is interesting to note that during infancy and childhood, despite the struggles with his wet nurse and being unable to digest his milk as a newborn, there is nothing negative written about Thomas' health, unlike his brother, Edmund, who is often described as *infirmatus* and who needed a physician's help at various intervals.[59] Maybe Thomas simply adjusted his behaviour depending on the rule at the time, treading that fine line mentioned earlier. As the 2006 study by Alison Marshall on Thomas shows, he may not have had the ability to ingratiate himself with his peers and collective political players of the ruling classes in the same way that his brother Edmund did, but there is some evidence he was a generous lord to his household and tenants, and it must be asked if Thomas acted any differently to other magnates of the time. He was generous to his household affinity, such as awarding manors, his tenants were not charged excessive rents and were free from tallage (a form of tax), and many of his retainers served him long term.

Thomas of Brotherton had been a benefactor of the Abbey of Bury St Edmunds and its defender. In October 1327 the king ordered Thomas and other officials to arrest and imprison the townsmen who had recently attacked the abbot and the convent – known as the Great Riot – imprisoning the abbey servants, killing fish in the fishponds, taking grass and trees from the meadows, and breaking the water conduit to the abbey.[60] The Brotherton coat of arms appears in the abbey gate, twice, and is thought to represent Thomas and his daughter, Margaret, as countess (the Gate was repaired after being damaged in the riot).[61]

Thomas was buried in the exalted position of the choir at the Abbey of Bury St Edmunds, which, like many others, was destroyed in the Dissolution of the Monasteries in 1539.

'Here sometime, under a goodly monument in the choir of this abbey church, lay interred the body of Thomas as, surnamed of Brotherton, the place of his birth, the fifth son of Edward I, after the conquest, king of England, by Margaret his second wife, the eldest daughter of Phillip king of France, surnamed the Hardy. He was created earl of Norfolk and made Earl Marshal of England by his half-brother, Edward II, which earldoms Roger Bigod (the last of that surname earl of Norfolk and earl Marshal) leaving no issue, left to the disposition of the king his father. This earl died in the year of our redemption 1338'.[62]

Interestingly, as late as 2001, in the village of Waldringfield, Suffolk – an hour south of Bungay and half an hour south of Framlingham – two bronze horse harness pendants were found, one with an enamelled shield shape with traces of the arms of Thomas of Brotherton and one plain gilded.[63]

Chapter 4

Edward II and the Norfolk Plantagenets

There is no way of knowing if Edward II ever met his niece, Alice of Norfolk. His reign was one of uncertainty, civil war and upheaval. Alice was only two or three years old at the time Edward was 'obliged to abdicate' in January 1327, the first king since the Norman Conquest to have done so. Her father's actions during the reign of Edward II may explain some descriptions of Thomas, such as being unpopular and incapable of being politically astute or significant. However, Thomas had to walk a fine line during this time, a line that came to an abrupt end for his brother Edmund, Earl of Kent, who was executed in 1330.[1]

Edward I's son and heir, Edward of Caernarvon – his youngest child and his only surviving son from his first marriage to Eleanor of Castile (1241–1290) – was born at Caernarvon Castle on 25 April 1284 during the close of Edward I's conquest of Wales. Edward of Caernarvon became heir to the throne of England, aged just four months old, after the death of his only surviving elder brother, Alfonso of Bayonne, in August 1284.[2]

In June 1305 Edward of Caernarvon – now the Prince of Wales – had a serious altercation with Walter Langton, the Bishop of Lichfield and Coventry, one of Edward I's most senior and loyal advisors. The altercation was serious enough for Edward I to cut off Prince Edward financially and from his courtiers, as well as banishing him to stay at Windsor Castle with just two servants. It is at this time we see that Prince Edward had a good relationship with his stepmother, Queen Marguerite, as did his sisters Joan of Acre (1272–1307), Elizabeth of Rhuddlan (1282–1316), and Mary of Woodstock (1279–1332). Elizabeth had been a constant companion of Queen Marguerite since

Thomas' traumatic birth in 1300 and both her and her sister Mary spent the summer of 1301 with Marguerite and attended the birth of Edmund of Woodstock that same August. Thomas would have known his much older half-sister Mary of Woodstock quite well; after Prince Edward's banishment to Windsor in 1305, the elaborate childhood household of both Thomas and Edmund had moved from Windsor later that summer to Ludgershall Castle in Wiltshire where Mary was their guardian.[3] The three royal sisters pleaded clemency with their father, Edward I, over the banishment of their brother, Prince Edward, with Mary offering for him to stay at her nunnery in Amesbury.[4] Joan of Acre, showing the most audacity and proof she did not stand in awe of her father, lent her brother Edward her royal seal, although he politely declined, probably rightly not wishing to further anger their father, and Elizabeth of Rhuddlan offered her brother financial assistance.[5]

Queen Marguerite also interceded on Edward's behalf with her husband, the king, in July 1305 regarding loosening the financial restraints on him.[6] In August Edward wrote to his sister Elizabeth that although he was well, he asked if Marguerite would intercede on his behalf to have two close friends returned to him, one being Piers Gaveston, a person whom most historians and authors agree was the ultimate cause of Edward's troubles at the beginning of his reign as king.[7] Piers Gaveston (unknown-1312) was the second son of a Gascony baron, Arnaud de Gabaston (various spelling variations), who had served Edward I for around twenty years before his death sometime before 1302. Piers had joined his father in the army of Edward I in 1297 in Flanders and then joined the household of Prince Edward around 1300 after impressing Edward I with his military prowess and sharp mind. Although his birth year is unknown and relatively little is known about his childhood, Piers is considered to have been of similar age and became confidante, best friend, and 'brother' to Edward II, setting the tone for the disaster that was to come.[8]

It has already been discussed how Prince Edward was cut off from his household during the summer of 1305, with Queen Marguerite interceding, and by October 1305 he was reconciled with his father.

In May of 1306, in anticipation of an approaching Scottish campaign, Prince Edward was knighted, along with 267 others, including Piers Gaveston and the likes of John Mowbray, grandfather to his namesake John Mowbray, future son-in-law of Margaret of Norfolk, in what was called The Feast of the Swans, a mass knighting ceremony and banquet – the largest in medieval England – and so-called because of two swans on a platter on which the vows were taken.[9] In October 1306, during this Scottish campaign, Piers, along with twenty or so other knights, left the battlefield without the king's permission, to go to France for jousting tournaments. Edward I was noted to be furious, and with Prince Edward continuing to ask for many favours for Piers, such as giving him the earldom of Cornwall and valuable land in Ponthieu, Piers Gaveston was banished into exile in February 1307.[10]

When Prince Edward became King Edward II in July 1307, aged twenty-three, he was noted as being tall, fair, and a 'very strong young man'.[11] He liked the company of commoners, including swimming with them, and on one occasion nearly drowning in the Fens, and his chamber accounts show that he paid fishermen in Doncaster to fish in his presence.[12] One of his first acts was to recall his favourite, Piers Gaveston, from exile, and he immediately made him Earl of Cornwall in his first charter as king, on 6 August 1307. Just three months later Edward II then arranged the marriage of his young niece, Margaret de Clare, second daughter of his sister, Joan of Acre, to Gaveston in November 1307 at Berkhamstead Castle, a property which he also gifted to Gaveston, thus bringing him into the royal family.[13]

When Edward II left Dover for France two months later, on 22 January 1308, to marry the twelve-year-old Isabella of France (c.1295–1358) – whose betrothal Edward I had arranged in 1299, along with his own to Marguerite of France, Isabelle's aunt – he left Gaveston as regent and keeper of the kingdom in his absence, causing the *Vita* to note that 'an exile was now a keeper of the land'. This caused growing resentment amongst the leading barons and magnates, such as the Earls of Warwick, Lincoln and Arundel amongst others, who were tiring of Gaveston's haughty ways and of Edward's favouritism towards him.

The magnates didn't forget that Gaveston was merely a former squire, a foreigner in their eyes, and therefore did not have their breeding.[14] Although one could expect a regent to be a son and heir, which Edward didn't have, a blood brother would also be a right choice, which would lead to Thomas of Brotherton. However, Thomas of Brotherton was merely seven years old at this point so not plausible and it could point to Edward II not wishing to put his very young brother in the spotlight when 'his magnates were showing signs of increasing dissatisfaction'.[15]

The Dowager Queen Marguerite was present at the wedding of her niece Isabella to Edward II, on 25 January 1308 in Boulogne, and it's quite possible she took the young Thomas and Edmund with her.[16] Marguerite's brother, King Philippe IV of France, lavished wedding gifts on Edward, who proceeded to send them onto Piers back in England. Much has been written about Edward sending on Isabella's wedding gifts, namely jewellery, for Piers to keep, and the anger and upset this caused, but as the historian Kathryn Warner has shown, the translation of the particular passage regarding this event, from the English medieval chronicle *Annales Paulini* – considered to have been written by a canon of St Paul's Cathedral in London during the 1330s – actually lists the gifts such as a luxury couch and war horses to Edward and Edward alone. It is quite within reason to send them back to his regent in England for safe keeping, but because of the growing resentment of Piers Gaveston, this statement, fired by 'malicious rumour', had more than likely fed into the escalating suspicion of the relationship and favouritism between Gaveston and Edward.[17] Edward and Isabella returned to Dover on 7 February 1308, with Edward allegedly singling out Gaveston for preferential treatment as soon as he landed; later narratives state how Isabella was bereft and offended at being ignored whilst Edward favoured greeting Piers the minute they disembarked. However, Isabella and Edward landed separately at Dover so it is highly unlikely Isabella was upset at something she couldn't have witnessed.[18] Gaveston did, however, take a presumptuous role in the coronation of Edward and Isabella on the 25 February 1308, offending both the French and English nobility by wearing the royal colour of purple and taking a leading role, as well as offending Isabella's family at the following banquet.[19]

This was the social backdrop as Thomas was growing into his place in baronial society.

In 1300 the earldom of Cornwall had reverted back to the Crown after the death of Edward I's cousin, Edmund of Cornwall, and the *Vita* notes that the king had intended the earldom – which had always been in the royal family – to be passed to either of his sons, Thomas or Edmund.[20] In 1302, Roger Bigod, then the Earl of Norfolk, had made Edward I his heir and all that the title entailed, as long as he died without issue, which he did in 1306.[21] In August 1306 Edward I made it clear in the patent rolls that the Norfolk lands and titles were to go to Thomas, his second son but first child with Marguerite, with land values of 7,000 marks going to the younger Edmund; also a settlement on their younger sister Eleanor, who sadly didn't survive childhood. There is no mention of the earldom of Cornwall.[22] When Bigod died in late 1306 the estates were managed by the Crown's ministers for the next six years; Edward II had his young brothers welfare to consider, such as sending them oaks for their fires from the royal forest during the winter of 1311, for example, and the earldom of Norfolk was granted to a twelve-year-old Thomas of Brotherton in December 1312 by Edward II, a month after the birth of his first child, a son and heir who would eventually become Edward III.[23]

The year 1312 was the year that saw the death of Piers Gaveston. Despite being ordered into a third exile in November 1311, Gaveston returned to England and travelled to York with Edward II around 13 January 1312, where his wife, Margaret, Countess of Cornwall, had given birth to their daughter, Joan, the previous day. On the 18 January 1312, in York, Edward II declared the return of the 'good and loyal' Piers Gaveston on the king's orders, that his exile had been 'contrary to law and custom', and promptly restored his lands – including the earldom of Cornwall – back to him.[24]

This prompted the excommunication of Gaveston in March 1312 by Archbishop Winchelsey, as per the Ordinances. These were a series of forty-one regulations against Edward II formulated by twenty-one of his leading barons and clergy who were 'powerful and discreet men of the whole kingdom';[25] they included the Archbishop of Canterbury, the bishops of London, Salisbury, Chichester, Norwich, St David's and Llandaff, the Earls of Lincoln, Pembroke, Gloucester, Lancaster, Hereford, Richmond, Warwick and Arundel, as well as Hugh de Vere, Robert Clifford, Hugh Courtney, William Marshall and William Martin.[26] These reforms were first drafted in 1310 and signed off by Edward in 1311 after his initial refusal to accept them, but the pressure on him was too much and he signed them off in September 1311. One of the regulations was that 'all evil counsellors should be expelled'. This was used to take aim at a number of persons, the top of the list being Gaveston, who was accused of 'having given the king bad counsel and led him into evil ways and accroached (usurped) royal power for himself'. Any friends or family were also ordered to be away from the king. On 19 May 1312 Gaveston was besieged at Scarborough Castle by the Earls of Pembroke and Warwick and agreed to their terms of proceeding with negotiations with Edward II regarding his influence. Gaveston was given safety in the custody of the Earl of Pembroke but was seized by the Earl of Warwick, condemned to death at Warwick Castle, and beheaded at a place called Blacklow Hill, en route to Kenilworth, belonging to Thomas, 2nd Earl of Lancaster, who was first cousin but mortal enemy to Edward II.[27]

The Dowager Queen Marguerite had retired shortly after the coronation of Edward and her niece, Isabella, in 1308. Although she had shared a good working relationship with Edward, proven by his letters to her asking for assistance with his banishment, for example, as well as his sisters, whispers were afoot of her possible involvement with her half-brother, Philippe IV of France. Talk of Marguerite sending money to aid the baronial rebellion against Gaveston[28], as well as passing sensitive information to Philippe, may indicate her concerns for her young niece, Queen Isabella, although it is possible Marguerite was looking at protecting her sons' interests and inheritances. The passing of sensitive information was first mentioned by the contemporary chronicler Sir Thomas Grey in his chronicle, *Scalacronica*, which wasn't written until 1355. In his book on Edward I, Michael Prestwich considers this event unlikely but maybe representative of the distrust surrounding Marguerite from the days of the unpopular marriage treaty between her and Edward I in 1299.[29] Marguerite doesn't appear much in the records after her retirement to Marlborough Castle in Wiltshire. Edward II confiscated her castles of Gloucester in October 1317 and Leeds and Berkhamsted in November 1317, although they were eventually restored to her.[30] Marguerite died on 14 February 1318. Her funeral at Greyfriars in London, a wealthy abbey she had endowed in the past, was attended by Edward II and Isabella as well as Mary of Woodstock. Her sons, Thomas and Edmund, were executors of her will and both were already in the service of Edward II, with Thomas having been called to Parliament in January 1313 in a complimentary role due to Thomas being only twelve years old at this point. In July 1319 Thomas of Brotherton was left as keeper of the realm when Edward II travelled to Scotland.[31]

Despite these honours and earlier support of his young brothers, Edward II wasn't particularly generous towards Thomas or Edmund, and by 1310 had only partially fulfilled the wishes of their father, Edward I, laid out in August 1306. In fact, Thomas' younger brother, Edmund, was only given the title Earl of Kent and lands in 1321.[32] Maybe Edward II had foreseen the need for the support of his two younger brothers; in January 1322 he had arrived in Shrewsbury, preparing for open conflict with his barons regarding yet another favouritism from the king to the Despensers, namely Hugh Despenser the Younger. Relations between Edward II and his barons had never really settled since the times of Gaveston and now Edward II was prepared to take his revenge. Despite the royalist earls, including Thomas of Brotherton, attempting to negotiate with the rebellious barons in February 1322, Edward II finally came to battle against the barons who were led by his cousin, Thomas, Earl of Lancaster, in March 1322 at Boroughbridge, resulting in a resounding success for the king, although the Earl of Lancaster's defeat could be seen as the result of desertions as opposed to a battle itself.[33] The author of the *Vita* also notes how 'His two brothers came to the lord king's help, namely Thomas, Earl Marshal, and Edmund, Earl of Kent, active soldiers considering their age.' Edmund, Earl of Kent, along with the Earl of Surrey, were ordered to lay siege to the Earl of Lancaster in March 1322 at his castle in Pontefract, where Lancaster, himself a cousin of Edward II as well as Thomas of Brotherton, was then executed.[34]

One of those killed at the Battle of Boroughbridge had also been one of the Ordainers in 1311. Humphrey Bohun, Earl of Hereford, was the brother-in-law of Thomas, being the husband of Elizabeth of Rhuddlan, with whom Thomas' mother, Dowager Queen Marguerite, had nurtured an enduring friendship over the years. Marguerite had been in attendance to Elizabeth at her wedding in November 1302 and Elizabeth's headdress was possibly a gift from Marguerite (it had belonged to Marguerite's sister, Blanche).[35] Elizabeth had also enlisted Marguerite's help in securing marriages for the daughters of her and Humphrey. Elizabeth died in childbirth in May 1316, with her newborn daughter dying shortly after.[36]

After the failure of the February 1322 negotiations, Thomas of Brotherton appears not to have taken part in any further actions of the civil war between Edward II and his barons, neither the battle at Boroughbridge nor the trial and execution at Pontefract of Thomas of Lancaster, his cousin as well as Edward II's, whereas his brother, Edmund, did. Norfolk had attempted to negotiate with the Mortimers, Roger and his uncle, and possibly disapproved of the way Edward II was conducting matters in the lead up to Boroughbridge. Between 1321 and 1322 Thomas witnessed no royal charters, as he had previously, and it seems Edward may not have trusted Thomas' complete loyalty; in November 1321 Thomas – but not Edmund – was a recipient of a letter forbidding him to attend an assembly called by the Earl of Lancaster: 'The like to the earls of Arundel, Surrey, Norfolk, and Athole, and to one hundred and two others.'[37] A rift appeared to be bubbling under the service between Thomas and Edward II, despite outward appearances of loyalty and seemingly being 'closely aligned with the court' with his brother Edmund.[38]

Interestingly, it was around this time of Thomas falling out of favour with Edward II that Thomas married far beneath his social position, and possibly had his first child, in defiance of the discussions Edward II was holding with the king of Aragon and the marriage of two of his daughters to Thomas and his own son, Prince Edward.[39] Thomas had to tread a fine line now. By the time Alice of Norfolk, his third and final child, was born in 1324, Edward II had another firm favourite in the form of Hugh Despenser the Younger, and tensions were again rising against Edward II's rule and Despenser's tyrannical influence. Queen Isabella departed for Paris in March 1325, acting as a diplomatic intercessor between her brother, the French King Charles IV, and Edward II. Intercessions were successful in laying a basis for discussions, although France wanted Edward II to pay homage. By August he had arrived in Dover, but claimed illness made him unable to travel, although many in France and England believed Despenser convinced him not to go:[40]

> But Hugh Despenser the son, not wanting anyone to advise the king to cross, on account of the imminent danger, is said to have remarked arrogantly to some: "Now it will become clear who advises the king to cross over to his enemies; since he is a manifest traitor whoever he may be." On hearing these threats the bishops and nobles answered the lord king's enquiry saying: "Lord, it is known that many great men of the realm are absent, and it is not fitting for us to give answer in so difficult a matter without our peers."[41]

It was agreed by all parties that the thirteen-year-old heir to the throne, Prince Edward, should sail to France in place of his father in September 1325, accompanied by his uncle and younger brother of Thomas of Brotherton, Edmund, Earl of Kent. However, although Queen Isabella refused to come home from Paris, stating her fear and anger of Despenser, she now had her trump card – her son the prince – in her possession.

The queen also had exiled earls by her side, including Alice of Norfolk's uncle, Edmund, Earl of Kent, as well as the powerful Marcher lord, Roger Mortimer. Mortimer had been in Paris since August 1323 after escaping from the Tower of London whilst under the watch of the constable Stephen Segrave, great-grandfather to Margaret of Norfolk's first husband. Queen Isabella's constant refusal to come home unless Despenser was removed, and Edward's refusal to remove him, meant that by Christmas 1325 fear of an invasion spearheaded by Isabella and Mortimer caused Edward II to reinforce castles back in England. Early in 1326 Isabella negotiated a deal with Count William II of Hainault who, in exchange for supplying her with a force of 700 mercenaries to be led by his brother, John, would also give his daughter, Philippa of Hainault, in marriage to the young Prince Edward.[42]

Around the same time, in January 1326, Edward II – accompanied by the ever-present Despenser – attempted a reconciliation of sorts with Thomas, vising him in Norfolk and employing Thomas' sister-in-law, Joan Jermy, as governess of his two younger daughters. Joan appears to have been a royal favourite, not purely just as governess, but was the recipient of gifted items such as clothing, soap, furs and a silver enamelled cup.[43] However, the visit was to no avail. It was obvious who Thomas of Brotherton supported when Isabella sailed from Holland on 22/23 September 1326 – with Mortimer, Edmund and John of Hainault along with many other exiles and their retinues – landing two days later on Suffolk estates owned by Thomas, who was one of the first magnates to greet her return. One can only wonder at Edward II's feelings of this defection by his brother. Although Edward II had ordered a fleet to be mustered against Isabella, it appears the sailors of England refused to do so due to the 'great wrath they had of Hugh Despenser'. Isabella and her invading force landed without any opposition.[44] Despenser's father, known as Hugh Despenser the Elder, advised Edward II that time was up for either hiding, running or battling Queen Isabella as she wouldn't have dared to land with such a small army if she wasn't confident of support in England.[45] Isabella had both aristocratic and ecclesiastical support after landing back on English soil, with London coming out in support of her, but her return did not pass without violence – the Bishop of Exeter, ally of Edward II, Walter Stapledon, was beheaded with a bread knife by a mob whilst trying to reach the safety of St Paul's, and two of his squires were also killed. Edward II, realising just what he was up against, offered pardons to most, but not all, felons willing to fight for him. By mid-October Despenser the Elder had left to defend his base of Bristol Castle, and the king, along with the catalyst of all his troubles, Hugh Despenser the Younger, was at Chepstow Castle. They sailed from there on 20 October, possibly heading for Lundy Island, which belonged to Despenser. Unfortunately, the fates, and weather, were against the small party and they were forced to anchor back in South Wales, at Cardiff, on 25 October, before making their way to Despenser's stronghold of Caerphilly Castle, arriving there on the 27 October.[46] By the time Queen Isabella had reached Gloucester, the northern armies had flocked to her cause and mustered at the city, including the army of Thomas, Lord Wake, brother-in-law to the Edmund, Earl of Kent and son-in-law to Henry, Earl of Lancaster, the king's cousin.[47]

Isabella's route from Gloucester to Bristol, where the elder Despenser held the mighty fortification of the castle and the town, was marred by incidences of violence and theft by her armies, with the reeves and bailiffs of the Berkeley estates raising complaints. Whilst passing through the villages of Slimbridge and Hurst – along the route that today would be recognised as the A38, the old Roman trading route[48] – the Earl of Lancaster's men were accused of stealing poultry, their horses ate all the oats and hay, and they damaged a chapel door. John of Hainault's men were accused of stealing oats and cattle, while Edmund, Earl of Kent, was accused of breaking the barn doors and stealing oats from within: 'Reeve of Wotton complaineth likewife of the Earle of Kents men, howe that in theire paffage with the Queene towards Briftoll, they brake his barnes doore, and wafted five quarters and an half of his oates.'(Berkeley Manuscripts).

The reeves and bailiffs also complained about their own lord, Thomas Berkeley, who rode his horses so hard to get to Bristol, and then Wales, in pursuit of the Despensers, that the mares miscarried, leaving no colts to store for that year. Ironically, Thomas Berkeley had joined Isabella and Mortimer at Gloucester and secured his castle of Berkeley for the young Prince Edward, so it was highly unlikely that the common people, already dealing with the economic struggles and environmental turmoil of the fourteenth century, would find any recompense for the loss of their supplies.[49]

On arrival at Bristol, there was no resistance and the city surrendered, with Depsenser the Elder now the soon-to-be-executed prisoner of Queen Isabella and Roger Mortimer. At Bristol Castle on 26 October 1326, a day after Edward II and Despenser had to put in at Cardiff, in front of a great assembly of archbishops, barons and knights, including his half-brothers, Thomas and Edmund, Edward II was accused of leaving his realm with the queen's enemies of Hugh Despenser the Younger and Robert Baldock, and Prince Edward was thus duly made guardian of the realm. Prince Edward is referred to as the Duke of Aquitaine during this ceremony, but as the Great and Privy Seals were with Edward II the prince's Privy Seal as the Duke of Aquitaine was used instead. This was given directly to Isabella's clerk, Robert Wyville, authorising her to act in her son's name:

> king Edward, son of king Edward, upon the said king going away from his realm of England with Hugh le Despenser, the younger, and Master Robert de Baldok, enemies of the queen, his consort, and of Edward, his eldest son, duke of Aquitaine, and other enemies of the queen and duke, the realm being left without rule, A. archbishop of Dublin, J. bishop of Winchester, J. bishop of Ely, H. bishop of Lincoln, A. bishop of Hereford and W. bishop of Norwich, and other prelates, and Sir Thomas, earl of Norfolk, Sir Edmund, earl of Kent, the king's brothers, and Henry, earl of Lancaster and Leicester, Thomas Wake, Henry de Bello Monte, William la Zousche of Assheby, Robert de Monte Alto, Robert de Morle, Robert de Watevill, and other barons and knights then at Bristol, in the presence of the queen and duke, with the assent

of the whole community of the realm there present, unanimously chose the duke keeper of the realm, so that the said duke and keeper should rule and govern the realm in the name and right of the king his father.[50]

On 27 October 1326, as Edward II and Despenser the Younger arrived at Caerphilly Castle, Despenser the Elder's mock trial sentenced him to death and he was duly executed outside Bristol Castle the same day. Denied any defence, Despenser the Elder was hung from public gallows with his body fed to dogs. His head was transported to Winchester (Despenser's earldom) on a spear for public display. On 16 November 1326 Edward II and Despenser the Younger were captured near Llantrisant, South Wales. Despenser was taken to Hereford, humiliated by villagers as they passed, and at his mock trial at Hereford on 24 November 1326 was found guilty of being a traitor, thief and an exile. He was semi-strangled, put onto a ladder where his heart was cut out, then disembowelled and then beheaded.[51] Edward II was under the care of his cousin, the Earl of Lancaster, who took him to his own castle of Kenilworth, arriving there by 5 December. Edward had been under house arrest at Monmouth Castle en route to Kenilworth, where he surrendered the Privy and Great Seal of England to the Bishop of Hereford, asking that it be used not just for right and peace but also 'for what pleased them'. Two months later, on 7 January 1327, Edward II was 'obliged to abdicate' and the new king, fourteen-year-old Edward III, was crowned on 1 Feb 1327 at Westminster Abbey.[52]

Life for Thomas, and Edmund especially, was about to get even harder.

Chapter 5

Edward III and the Norfolk Plantagenets

February 1327. England may have a new king, but due to his minority the new regime was Queen Isabella with her main aide, Roger Mortimer. Over the next three years this regime came to be hated as much as the Gaveston and Despenser sagas had been previously.

Roger Mortimer is generally assumed to have become Queen Isabella's lover at some point during their *de facto* rule. Who exactly was Roger Mortimer? Born at Wigmore Castle, Hereford, in 1287, Roger Mortimer was the firstborn son and heir of a powerful Marcher Lord, Edmund, 2nd Baron Mortimer of Wigmore, and his wife, Margaret Fiennes. Wigmore Castle had been built in 1067 by William FitzOsbern, close friend of William the Conqueror, and one of the warriors of 1066. He was also the builder of the original motte and bailey castles of Chepstow, Monmouth and Hereford, amongst others.[1] FitzOsbern was killed in battle at Flanders in 1071 with his son and heir falling foul of William I, who subsequently gave Wigmore Castle to another of his faithful supporters, Ralph (also known as Ranulph) Mortimer in 1075. The Mortimers held this castle until Roger Mortimer's execution in 1330, and was not returned to the family until 1342, by which time Ludlow Castle had become the Mortimer family seat. Ludlow had come to Roger Mortimer through his wife, Joan de Geneville, an extremely wealthy heiress of the Welsh Marches and of lands in Ireland, her two younger sisters having been placed in Acornbury Priory by their grandfather, who was acting against his estates being broken up between the three sisters. Joan, as the eldest, became the sole heiress, and then in 1314 the *suo jure* Baroness Geneville after the death of her grandfather (her father had died in 1292). Born in 1286 and married, aged fifteen, to the fourteen-year-old Roger Mortimer in September 1301, Joan and Roger had twelve surviving children, one of whom, Beatrice, would marry the young Edward of Norfolk, Alice's brother. After his death, by 1334, she had married Thomas Braose. Roger and Joan's marriage appears to have been a close and companionable one until at least 1322.[2]

In 1320 Roger Mortimer and his uncle, Mortimer of Chirk, the justiciar of Wales, had joined other magnates with Welsh interests such as Hugh Audley, Roger Damory, John Mowbray, Humphrey Bohun and John Giffard in rising against the continuing avarice and power of Hugh Despenser the Younger in Wales. Mortimer also had support of 30,000 native Welsh people who had suffered at the hands of Despenser.[3] Then in June 1321, Roger Mortimer was at an assembly called by Thomas, 2nd Earl of Lancaster and first cousin to Thomas of Brotherton, where discussions were held regarding defending the realm against attack by the Scots. They also drew up an indenture 'in the name of some sixty magnates whereby they pledge themselves to secure the destruction of the Despensers'.[4] In August 1321 the Marcher lords successfully bought about the banishment and exile of both Hugh Despenser the Younger and his father, Hugh the Elder, in which Mortimer had been a major player, and ordered that the port of Dover was to be the only port that the Despensers can 'void and pass out from the realm' between 14 and 29 August, finishing with 'And if they stay in the realm of England after that day, or if they return afterwards, they shall be treated as enemies of the king and of the realm.'[5] Shortly after, on 20 August 1321, there followed a general pardon by Edward II to all those involved including Mortimer and many of his retinue involved in the devastation of the Despenser lands.[6]

However, just two months later, in October, Queen Isabella was refused entry to Leeds Castle, Kent, the stronghold of Bartholomew Badlesmere (one of the contrariants mentioned in the last chapter), giving Edward II enough reason to raise an army against this insult. Thomas of Brotherton and others such as the Earl of Pembroke led the armies, with the king himself arriving on 25 October. Mortimer responded to Badlesmere's pleas for help, along with others, but the castle had fallen to the king and his army. The Earl of Lancaster ordered that no one was to help Badlesmere, and summoned another meeting of magnates at Doncaster on 29 November 1321. Edward II sent out letters on 12 November to over one hundred magnates warning them not to attend 'an assembly without his licence'; those named included Thomas, Earl of Lancaster, Humphrey de Bohun, Earl of Hereford and Essex, and the Earls of Arundel, Surrey, Norfolk, and Atholl.[7] The fact that Norfolk got a letter and his brother, Edmund, didn't was maybe a sign that Edward II did not have complete trust in Norfolk's loyalty; Thomas was, after all, a Marcher lord with his lordship of Chepstow. He had also married in August, without the king's consent, which couldn't have helped Edward's mood towards him. However, by the end of the year the Despensers had been recalled and Roger Mortimer and his uncle, Mortimer of Chirk, after losing much of their Welsh strongholds and allies, subsequently surrendered to the king at Shrewsbury in January 1322. Both were sent to the Tower of London. Mortimer of Chirk, being in his seventies at this point, died whilst a prisoner, but Roger Mortimer escaped in August 1323, as we saw previously, by drugging the constable, Stephen Segrave, and his guards and fled to France where he joined Queen Isabella.

Queen Isabella had accomplished what no other person had since the Conquest – she had displaced an anointed king with the aid of many disgruntled magnates and those in exile with her, such as the Earl of Kent, Alice's uncle, and Roger Mortimer. Isabella's son was now the rightful, albeit underage, king and a regency council was set up, headed by Henry, Earl of Lancaster, and including the young king's uncles, Thomas and Edmund. But it was a council in name only, with no real power to rule, and Mortimer decided to keep assuming power for himself. By 1328 the avaricious Mortimer had granted lands and lordships previously held by the Despensers and Arundel to himself, created himself Earl of March, as well as holding tournaments so rich they equalled that of the king. Mortimer was acting every inch a royal member, much to the horror of the regency council. He knew the queen depended on him, and the young king was under his control, thus, over the next couple of years,

Remains of Bungay Priory, in the churchyard of St Mary's. Burial place of its founder, Countess Gundreda, and highly likely the last resting place of Alice of Norfolk. (© *Ashley Dace at geography.co.uk by CC BY-SA 2.0*)

Another view of the remains of Bungay Priory. (© *Ashley Dace at geography.co.uk by CC BY-SA 2.0*)

Remains of the entrance towers of Bungay Castle. Birthplace of Alice's youngest child, Joan Montagu, future countess of Suffolk, home to Alice and place of her attack and eventual death. (© *Ashley Dace at geography.co.uk by CC BY-SA 2.0*)

A view from inside Bungay Castle, looking towards the inside of the towers with remains of what was once a huge Keep over 100ft tall and wall up to 7m thick on the right, and remains of a building that housed stairs. See britainexpress.co.uk for more information. (© *Ashley Dace at geography.co.uk by CC BY-SA 2.0*)

Remains of the once mighty Keep at Bungay Castle. (© *Ashley Dace at geography.co.uk by CC BY-SA 2.0*)

Model of what Bungay Castle would have looked like. Note the model of St Mary's and area of Bungay Priory to the top left and the distinctive round tower in the top left corner of Holy Trinity Church. (© *Ashley Dace at geography.co.uk by CC BY-SA 2.0*)

Holy Trinity Church, mentioned in the Domesday Book, and has the Montagu and Brotherton Arms in the stonework. (© *Adam Tinworth at flickr.com by CC BY-ND 2.0*)

View from the top of St Mary's Church, showing priory remains and facing Trinity Street. (© *Ned Nesbitt at geography.co.uk by CC BY-SA 2.0*)

Framlingham Castle, seat of Thomas of Brotherton and eventually Margaret of Norfolk. (© *Keith Evans at geograph.co.uk by CC BY-SA 2.0*)

Remains of the Abbey of Bury St Edmunds, final resting place of Thomas of Brotherton, Earl of Norfolk. (© *Bob Jones at geography.co.uk by CC BY-SA 2.0*)

Remains of what was the large Keep of Wark Castle, where Edward Montagu was the likely castellan in early 1342 and where Alice of Norfolk was with him. (© *Walter Baxter at geograph.co.uk by CC BY-SA 2.0*)

The magnificent Caerphilly Castle as seen today, with its famous leaning tower. Where Edward II fled to with Hugh Despenser the Younger after Queen Isabella and Roger Mortimer's invasion to reclaim the crown in the name of Edward II's son, the lord Edward, future Edward III. (© *Louise Wyatt. All Rights Reserved*)

Corbels of Edward II (facing outward) and Queen Isabella inside the Great Hall at Caerphilly Castle. (© *Louise Wyatt. All Rights Reserved*)

Remains of the Great Tower at Monmouth Castle. Where the husband of Joan of Acre, Gilbert the Red de Clare, died suddenly in 1295. Also the place where Edward II resigned his Great Seal and Privy Seal to the Bishop of Hereford in 1326 and the birthplace of Henry V sixty years later, in 1386. (© *Louise Wyatt. All Rights Reserved*)

The garden precinct within the hollowed out remains of Greyfriars Monastery in London. Hard to imagine this is the burial place of Queen Marguerite, grandmother to Alice of Norfolk, Queen Isabella, wife of Edward II and Margaret of Norfolk. (© *Marathon at geograph.co.uk by CC BY-SA 2.0*)

Memorial stone to Simon Montagu, older brother to Edward. (© *Andrewrabbott at Wikipedia by CC BY-SA 3.0*)

Remains of tomb marking the spot where Walter Mauny was reburied in the remaining grounds of the priory he founded, now known as London Charterhouse. (*Image reproduced with kind permission of © Brad Verity, all rights reserved*)

What is left of Clare Priory, Suffolk, final resting place of Joan of Acre, with her son Edward by her infamous second marriage to Ralph Monthermer. (© *Andrew Abbott at geograph.co.uk by CC BY-SA 2.0*)

Ruins of an early-sixteenth-century building known as Magor Mansion, also known as Procurator's House. A procurator was a court official dealing with the law and all things financial. On the site of a former house mentioned in the fourteenth century in relation to Tintern Abbey (the house is next to the parish church). This is likely to be where the king's court was held when Margaret of Norfolk was taken to task regarding her mob-handed dealings with the people of the surrounding areas and her claim to the jurisdiction of her manor, lands and castle of Chepstow. (© *Colin Smith at geograph.co.uk by CC BY-SA-2.0*)

Bungay entry in Domesday Book of 1086, showing it was the largest settlement in the area at 215 households. (*Image courtesy of Professor John Palmer, George Slater at opendomesday.org by CC BY-SA 3.0*)

V.
English Banners at Crecy.

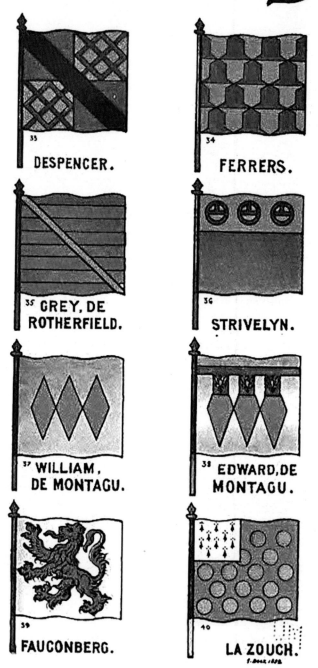

DESPENCER.

FERRERS.

35 GREY, DE ROTHERFIELD.

36 STRIVELYN.

37 WILLIAM, DE MONTAGU.

38 EDWARD, DE MONTAGU.

FAUCONBERG.

LA ZOUCH.

Images of just some of the coat of arms of the warriors at Crecy. See *Crecy and Calais* by George Wrottesley, pV. Note the arms of Edward Montagu next to that of his nephew William.

Tomb of Elizabeth Montfort, Lady Montagu, mother of Edward Montagu and guardian of his two youngest daughters after his attack on Alice of Norfolk. (*Image by Pruneau at Wikipedia Commons in the public domain*)

The Troops of Lord Montacute in the Subterranean Passage.

1865 sketch of William Montagu's men using the secret tunnel for the Nottingham Castle Coup of 1330. Edward Montagu was most likely one of these men. (*Image courtesy of* Cassell's Illustrated History of England Vol I, *p367*)

One of the three surviving and much renovated Eleanor Crosses. (© *Amanda Slater at flickr.com by CC BY-SA 2.0*)

1865 sketch of a young Queen Philippa arriving in London for her coronation on 17 February 1330. Both Thomas of Brotherton and his brother Edmund escorted Philippa on either side of her horse, holding the bridle dressed as grooms and can be seen drawn here [ODNB]. (*Image courtesy of* Cassell's Illustrated History of England Vol I, *p361*)

Reception of Philippa of Hainault at London.

Remains of Ludgershall Castle, Wiltshire. Summer residence of Thomas of Brotherton as a young boy and where he would have enjoyed frequent visits by his aunt, the nun-princess Mary of Woodstock. (*© Colin Smith at geograph.co.uk by CC BY-SA 2.0*)

he proceeded to take land, especially in the Marcher borders, and made sure his men were main keyholders throughout the kingdom. In 1325 Mortimer had seen his cousin, Margaret Wake (c.1297–1349) married to Edmund, and as he had made himself an earl in 1328, he could expect his children to marry the offspring of other earls. Mortimer exploited his valuable wardship of the young heir to the earldom of Pembroke, Laurence Hastings, by marrying him to his daughter Agnes, and another daughter, Beatrice, to Edward of Norfolk, the only son and heir of Thomas, Earl of Norfolk. To celebrate this double wedding, in 1329 Mortimer held an elaborately themed round table tournament, which saw him crowned King Arthur, with Isabella his Guinevere. None of this went down well. His familiarity was offensive, and even his own son, Sir Geoffrey Mortimer, called him the 'King of Folly'.[8]

By September 1329 tensions had grown between the young Edward III and the regime of his mother and Mortimer to such a degree that he sent his loyal companion and trusted friend, William Montagu – elder brother of Edward Montagu, who married Alice of Norfolk – to the Pope in Avignon informing him of the events in England. Edward III gave reassurances to the Pontiff that only Montagu and Richard Bury, his secretary, knew the password *pater sancte* ('holy father'), which would guarantee that correspondence would be from only him and not Mortimer or Isabella acting in his name.[9]

Then, in early 1330, Thomas of Brotherton suffered a personal tragedy with the death of his younger brother, Edmund, aged just twenty-nine. Of course, there is no way of knowing how Thomas personally felt at the loss of his brother, but given they were only a year apart in age, had their own shared household from 1301 until 1312, and were hardly apart (as well as occasionally acting in conjunction politically), it's fair to say Edmund's death would have, at the very least, caused some emotional turmoil for Thomas. Together on a daily basis from when they were born, they had completed an education together that would prepare them for life as royal magnates: riding, hunting and military prowess, religious studies, becoming adept at chess (an activity that was more than the board game we consider it today, a study in logical manoeuvres and emblematic of the higher society into which they were born). Their household sheriff, servants and caregivers of their formative years were shared until they were young adults.[10]

Edmund was executed on 19 March 1330 for his part – along with others such as his brother-in-law, Thomas Wake, Sir Fulk Fitzwarin, a Marcher lord knighted with Edward II in 1306, and Sir John Gymmynges who had been a valet of Edward II – of a plot to free the deposed Edward after rumours circulated that he was still alive, and take him to Edmund's castle of Arundel and then, presumably, abroad by boat supplied by Gymmynges and gold offered by William Melton, Archbishop of York.[11] At his trial, Edmund only named a few of the men involved, although on 31 March 1330, twelve days after his execution, the government ordered the arrest of forty-one others.[12] It is interesting to note that Thomas of Brotherton was not mentioned anywhere, either in Edmund's confession or the order for more arrests, and he was not implicated in the plot to free Edward. It is highly likely Thomas was in Edmund's confidence, but Edmund would refuse to break his loyalty and name him, even it was by association only. The fact that Mortimer's daughter Beatrice was married to Thomas' son, Edward, may have also played a large part in saving Thomas from any implication as that would have meant Edward of Norfolk being disinherited.[13] It is probably no coincidence that shortly after his brother's execution, Thomas left England, on 16 April 1330, seemingly for the remainder of the year: 'Thomas, earl of Norfolk and marshal of England, going to Gascony on the king's service, has letters nominating Richard de Burghstede and Richard Dykene his attorneys until Christmas. The same earl has other letters nominating Robert de Aspale and Roger de Hales.'[14] However, Thomas must have been back in England by July, as he was being summoned to a colloquium in July 1330 and also in September.[15] Thomas was also entrusted with overseeing the trial and execution of Mortimer in November 1330.[16]

The act of the swift execution of Edmund ordered by Mortimer was the beginning of his downfall. There appears to have been widespread shock and condemnation that Edmund, a royal earl, was condemned to be executed in such a manner and the act was deemed so abhorrent that men at arms and their captains refused to comply. There was no one who would agree to commit the act of beheading Edmund. After a few hours of Edmund being made to wait for his own execution, Mortimer agreed to pardon a felon from his death penalty in exchange for his freedom and it was he who swung the axe.[17] However, rumours questioning the legality and manner in which Edmund had died still persisted, and on 13 April 1330 a writ was issued in the name of the king (but probably by Queen Isabella and Mortimer) that the king 'orders several sheriffs and the justiciary of Wales to proclaim the death of Edmund, late Earl of Kent, and to arrest those who say he was unjustly put to death'. Inquisitions were also held in Norfolk and Suffolk to uncover adherents to the late Earl of Kent.[18]

Mortimer showed no fear or remorse for executing a younger brother of Edward II, uncle to Edward III, a royal blooded Plantagenet. However, fear escalated in the aftermath of Edmund's execution, and the young King Edward III appears to have been motivated to act sooner rather than later in getting his regency under his own control, especially as his young wife, Queen Philippa, was pregnant. Mortimer also knew Edward was fast approaching his majority and had placed spies everywhere in the young king's household, and though he was aware of a plot by Edward III to overthrow the regency, he was unaware of the details.

Mortimer, Isabella and Edward III moved to Nottingham Castle in September 1330 and a great council was convened for 15 October 1330, seemingly for 'certain arduous affairs touching the king and the state of the realm and the king's other lands which have newly emerged.'[19] Mortimer ended up questioning Edward III's close friend and confidante William Montagu, as well as the king's close circle of friends, none of whom betrayed Edward III, and the plot to overthrow Mortimer and Isabella was put into action on the night of 19 October 1330. With the aid of local knowledge, and his tight band of brothers, including William Montagu, Robert Ufford, William Clinton, Ralph Stafford and Edward Bohun, Edward III had Roger Mortimer arrested in a coup that had seen the small group of Edward's loyal servants return to Nottingham Castle later that night under cover of darkness. They were led through a secret passage in the castle shown to them by a local man, then attacked Mortimer's men and arrested Mortimer. A month shy of his eighteenth birthday, Edward III was finally king in his own right.[20]

Although Thomas wasn't involved in the coup, it must be considered he had knowledge of the plot, just as Mortimer himself had. In September 1330 Thomas was one of those summoned to attend the council of 15 October, along with eight other earls, namely Cornwall, Lancaster, Surrey, Oxford, Hereford, March, Atholl from Scotland, and Warwick.[21] Although Thomas wasn't directly involved, Robert Ufford, one of his retainers, was, and as we saw in an earlier chapter, Ufford was later pardoned for the deaths of two of Mortimer's men. It is highly likely Edward Montagu also took part in the coup as he was in his brother William's retinue at the time. Ufford's son and heir, William, would go on to marry Thomas' granddaughter Joan Montague, Alice's youngest daughter.[22]

Thomas was again included on writs of summons for a council issued on 23 October 1330, along with the Earls of Cornwall, Lancaster, Surrey, Richmond, Oxford, Hereford, Warwick and Atholl, also the Archbishop of Canterbury and York, nineteen bishops, forty-seven barons and various other judges and clerks. On 26 November 1330 this council sat in on judgement of Mortimer, including charges of procuring the death of Edmund, Earl of Kent, usurping royal power and having Edward II moved to Berkeley Castle and having him murdered, amongst many others. Overseen by Thomas, Mortimer was judged as a traitor, with no defence, and was dragged to the gallows to be executed as a common criminal at Tyburn on 29 November 1330. Shortly before he was hung from the gallows, he admitted that Edmund, Earl of Kent had been a victim of a conspiracy. Marble arch now sits near the spot of the Tyburn Tree, a nickname for the gallows established in the twelfth century.[23]

The story of Edward II's murder (or non-murder) is a long and complicated one, recognisable by the well-known tale of Edward II being supposedly killed by a red-hot poker inserted into his bowels at Berkeley

Castle, where he was being held in September 1327. Thankfully, this has now more or less been debunked. There is no official record of the cause of death, including no mention of it in Edward III's Parliament of November 1330, so only the chronicles exist to state that particular sordid tale. It was first mentioned in the mid-1330s (after 1333) as a 'red-hot copper rod' and this was copied over the next few decades. However, most chronicles state various methods of his death, including Edward II being suffocated, strangled or just simply dying. And although the chronicles all agreed his life was extinguished at Berkeley Castle, it is debatable if Edward II even died in September 1327. One theory has him living his days out in anonymity in Italy.[24] This theory appears to stem from the letter of his custodian at the time of his official death at Berkeley Castle, Sir Thomas Berkeley, and whereby Edmund Earl of Kent and his adherents believed passionately enough to think Edward II was still alive. Edmund had, in fact, support from some powerful people, including the Bishop of London, Archbishop of York, the Earl of Mar, Sir John Pecche, Sir William de Zouche, a cousin of Roger Mortimer, and various clerks and monks, among many others.[25]

It would be nice to think of Edmund of Woodstock, Earl of Kent having the last laugh, being the grandfather of Richard II, who succeeded Edward III as king through Edmund's daughter, Joan of Kent.

Much has been written about Edward III's preference for his elevation of 'new men' to the peerage and nobility, mainly centred on his close circle of friends and knights who had helped him in the Nottingham coup and the overthrow of Mortimer.

As it was, the nobility was in something of a crisis by 1330; the executions and deaths in battles during the previous decade had led to a decline in male heirs and lineage failure. Between 1300 and 1325 the male line had died out in fifteen families, and by 1330 many of the titled nobility were either of an older generation or infirm, which is where Thomas of Brotherton sat, along with his cousin, the powerful Henry of Lancaster, 3rd Earl of Lancaster, who was becoming debilitated and losing his sight by 1330.[26] In fact, by 1330 Thomas was one of the last living remaining earls that had been created between 1307 and 1326.[27]

Edward III needed to replenish his Parliament and peerage – he would need new blood and new loyalty if he was to govern competently. This mode of harnessing new men wasn't ground-breaking; Henry I had also engaged men from obscure origins, men who had proven loyal in helping Henry take control of his monarchy and were rewarded with wealth and promotion up the ranks of the king's service. In his first decade of kingship, Edward III promoted nineteen men to the baronage and created seven new earls.[28] Those elevated to earldoms were those usually closest to him and, as well as having links to the Norfolk Plantagenets, were also able to bring some wealth to their new status. One of these was Robert Ufford (1298–1369) who became the 1st Earl of Suffolk; he was also the future father-in-law to Alice's daughters, Elizabeth and Joan. The Uffords had associations with the royal household going back to the 1240s and Robert had been a ward in the household of Edward II. He had become a close companion to Edward III during the regime of Queen Isabella and Mortimer, and as we have seen, was a main conspirator involved in the Nottingham coup of 1330.[29]

Probably the most well-known of these new men was William Montagu. More of the Montagu family will be discussed in the next chapter, but for now we'll see how Edward III's childhood friend and companion was associated with the Norfolk Plantagenets.

The Montagus, a west country land-owning family, had a strong link of royal household history, tracing their lineage back to the Norman conquest; there was a William Montagu attached to King John but dismissed in the rebellion of 1215. Simon, 1st Baron Montagu (c.1259–1316) had been keeper of Corfe Castle and had an impressive military career under Edward I. His son, William, 2nd Baron Montagu (c.1285–1319) had been seneschal of Gascony and had married in c.1292 Elizabeth Montfort, daughter of Sir Piers Montfort of Warwick, and it was Elizabeth who, in 1352, was given custody of her two young granddaughters, Maud and Joan, after the death of their mother, Alice of Norfolk. William and Elizabeth's second but first surviving son, Edward III's close childhood friend and companion William Montagu (1301–

1344), 3rd Baron Montagu, was under-age when his father, William, died in 1319, so was made a ward of Edward II in 1319, and later that year became part of the royal household as yeoman. The following years saw his companionship grow with the young prince, the future Edward III, and it was William who led the men during the Nottingham coup of 1330, thus helping secure the throne for Edward.[30]

Families with established household connections that went back generations, and who had a court presence as well as familial and personal ties within the nobility, usually found it easier for cadet branches of the family – namely younger sons – to be supported by the elder members and/or heirs of their dynastic families. The Montagu family were typical of this, with William becoming the 1st Earl of Salisbury, and so we find his two younger brothers doing very well thanks to William's connections. Simon (d.1345) became Bishop of Worcester then Ely, and the youngest, Edward Montagu, became noted for his military career, including Crécy, but found his brother's connections also made it possible to marry above his station, namely the high-born Alice of Norfolk, the younger daughter of the king's uncle, Thomas Earl of Norfolk.[31]

Another new man with not such a household background was Walter Mauny (sometimes spelt Manny). Born c.1310, he came over to England in 1327 as a page in the retinue of Philippa of Hainault, daughter of the count of Hainault (an area now on the border of Belgium and France), the new queen of England and wife to Edward III. He was recognised for his soldiering, bravery, and loyalty, rising up the ranks as one of the new men by being knighted in 1331, appointed keeper of Harlech Castle in Wales in 1332, and admiral of the North in 1337, as well as grants of landed estates across Buckinghamshire and Norfolk. He was also a retainer of Thomas of Brotherton and Thomas appointed Mauny as serjeanty of the king's Marshalsea of his household for the duration of his life.[32]

Walter Mauny, as previously discussed, went on to marry Alice's sister, the widowed Margaret of Norfolk, without the king's permission. He became highly regarded and respected, and when he died in 1372 at Margaret of Norfolk's Great Chesterton estate in Essex, his funeral was attended by the king and all of the kings' sons as well as many nobles, showing the esteem in which he was held.[33] The chronicler Le Bel (c.1290–1370), himself in the retinue of John of Hainault in 1327, wrote of Walter Mauny: 'nor should we forget Sir Walter Mauny, whose many feats of arms and prowess in Scotland and elsewhere had earned him such favour with the king and all the English, great and small, that the noble king had taken him into his innermost council and granted him such great estates in England that he was now a banneret, of higher status indeed than any other there.'[34]

In these three men, Robert Ufford, William Montagu and Walter Mauny, we see Thomas of Brotherton integrating with the seeds of the new nobility, Edward III's favourites. Young, virile and warrior-like, it was common sense to be part of them. Robert Ufford was a retainer in Thomas' household and after Thomas' death Robert's two sons would marry his granddaughters, Alice's daughters Elizabeth and Joan. William Montagu, we have seen, negotiated the hand of Alice of Norfolk originally to his son and heir, so an important match, and for reasons unknown married Montagu's younger brother, Edward, instead. Some of Thomas' actions at this time, such as signing away of lands and the valuable Chepstow lordship for example, have been considered the actions of a foolish, simple man who was taken for granted. However, could it be more a case of treading a fine line and winning? Did Thomas tread carefully amongst the politics and warring factions of the day, given what happened to his brother? As Marshall states in her study on Thomas (2006): 'Since Norfolk was one of few English earls created between 1307 and 1326 not to have been executed for treason by 1330, tendency to disassociate himself from the centre of politics was perhaps the most sensible course to take.'[35]

We know Alice was betrothed to William Montagu, heir to the earldom of Salisbury, in early 1333, although married to his uncle Edward at least by August 1338, around the time of the Brotherton's disorderly household. Alice must have met her cousin the king at some point, more than likely at her wedding, although nothing, not even the date of her wedding, is recorded. However, there is an incident recorded, albeit an enigmatic one, of Edward III taking a lustful shine to the wife of the castellan of Wark Castle during a Scottish campaign between December 1341 and January/February 1342. This appears to have only been written and discussed about in the 1983 biography of Edward III by Michael Packe. There are some errors, assumptions, and flowery writing in Packe's book, but it is a good starting point to examine whether this lady at Wark Castle was, in fact, Alice of Norfolk. A further rumour later the same year, August 1342, was that Edward III had become infatuated and subsequently raped the Countess of Salisbury, and both this and the Wark episodes were spuriously linked by chroniclers. In fact, they should be considered two completely separate incidents, and although the rape story is now more or less dismissed by modern historians as wartime French propaganda – and it does indeed appear to be a fabricated story – it is worth mentioning here as it is one of the rare occasions that Alice of Norfolk's appearance in records doesn't include land or property transactions. However, the focus here will be on the Wark Castle incident, a story that comes courtesy of the contemporary chronicler Jean le Bel and adapted from the translation by Nigel Bryant (2011).

Wark Castle sat on the River Tweed at the Scottish borders, with some minimal remains visible today, including the old keep. The modern village sits in what was once the castle bailey. Built near a ford in the river by Walter Espec (d.1153) in the early twelfth century, and due to its location near the English-Scottish border, Wark Castle has been ruined and rebuilt many times. As early as 1138, an attack was launched by King David of Scotland, who was attempting to capture the kingdom of Northumbria during the Anarchy of 1138–1153, which raged in England between King Stephen and his cousin, Empress Matilda. Walter Espec was one of Henry I's 'new men', as mentioned earlier, and he also founded Kirkham Priory and Rievaulx Abbey. He died around 1153 and left no heirs. King John passed the castle to the Ros (sometimes spelt Roos) family around 1200, although during the Baron's War and whilst marching north, King John attacked and ruined Wark Castle because Sir Robert de Ros was a signatory to the Magna

Carta. It is the unsuccessful siege of Wark Castle in early 1342 by the Scots that is relevant to the story regarding Alice.[36]

During a truce of a Scottish campaign in December 1341, Edward III stayed over in the Cornhill Manor, Northumberland, whilst making his way back south.[37] This was close to Wark Castle, which belonged to his friend William Montagu, 1st Earl of Salisbury. William was being held captive at this time, in France, along with Ufford. He had been held prisoner since April 1340 and had come close to being executed.[38] According to le Bel, the castellan of Wark was his nephew, another William, with the Countess of Salisbury in residence. It was the supposed nephew, William Junior, who saw the passing Scots army en route to Carlisle, and when he realised they were not going to attack, he stealthily rode out with sixty men at arms, overtook their rear baggage train at the edge of a nearby wood, and killed more than 200 men before taking their horses back to Wark Castle.[39] The Scots retaliated by marching back to Wark, besieging the castle the next day. According to le Bel, the 'valiant noble lady of Salisbury kept spirits high,' and 'the valiant lady gave constant encouragement'. It became apparent the garrison would need help, and knowing the king was not too distant, William Junior gave a speech to the garrison, understanding they did not want to leave the castle or its noble lady, but he himself would leave in the night to get to the king. Darkness fell and apparently the weather was bad, so it was relatively easy to make it past the sheltering and sleeping Scots, killing two Scottish soldiers who were making their way back to camp with oxen. When William Junior arrived at York (we now know that is wrong as wardrobe accounts show the king was at Cornhill around the time of the Scottish incursion into Northumberland), he explained the plight of the countess at the castle to the king and Edward III left the next day for Wark with 6000 men-at-arms, 10,000 archers and 80,000 foot. When he arrived at noon, the Scots had decamped and left for Jeburgh forest that morning after hearing Edward III was on his way, so the king and his men set up camp by the castle. Edward, with twelve of his knights, went to see the noble lady 'whom he hadn't seen since her wedding day'.[40]

By all accounts, when the noble lady (we still don't know her name) greeted the king at the gates with eternal thanks, both he and his men were astounded by her beauty. The king 'could not take his eyes off her: he was sure he'd never seen a more beautiful lady'. Abiding by etiquette, this noble lady with no name fed and entertained her royal visitor and his men, although Edward III did not eat or drink a great deal. Whilst some assumed it was frustration because the Scots had fled by the time he arrived, le Bel states it was due to the king's love (probably more likely lust) for the noble lady: 'his men were astonished, they were not used to seeing him like this'.[41] Edward left the next day to chase the Scots, to no avail, but did not pass by Wark on the return, instead sending the young William Montagu with a message to his aunt, the lady of Wark, that she should rejoice as he had her husband's welfare in mind. Later in the chronicle, Jean le Bel then states, 'And you've also heard of his [Edward III] passionate love for the valiant lady of Salisbury, named Alice'.[42] This is the first mention of her name. Six months or so after the Wark incident, the king organised a huge feast to celebrate the marriage of his son, Prince Lionel, in London, on 15 August 1342, to last for fifteen days: 'he summoned every lord, baron, knight, squire and all ladies and damsels to attend without excuse if they truly loved him: he commanded the earl of Salisbury (who had returned from captivity in June 1342) to ensure his wife was there and that she should bring with her all the ladies and damsels that she could find.'[43] The Countess of Salisbury apparently dressed demurely to avoid the king's attention, to no avail. Shortly afterwards, after sending the Earl of Salisbury on a mission to Brittany, he visited the countess at her castle where he allegedly raped her. Then Edward III left for Brittany, returning with the Earl of Salisbury, whereby the countess told her husband the details. He left in anger at the king, dividing his estates and leaving to fight abroad, where he died.[44]

Except he didn't. William Montagu died at a tournament at Windsor in January 1344. There is also no record of him falling out with the king, dividing his estates and going abroad. In fact, William Montagu continued on missions for the king until his untimely death. What is truth and what isn't? To help separate fact from fiction here, the 1976 study of the alleged rape by Antonia Gransden, as well as the analysis by Dr Ian Mortimer in his book *A Perfect King*, have been utilised alongside the charters to piece together, as best as can be, of what happened.

Wark Castle was indeed a Salisbury property, having been awarded to William Montagu for life in 1329, and held in *fee tail*, meaning the property could not be sold off and only passed down to an heir, thus in 1333 Wark Castle, manor, lands, forests, warrens, fairs, advowsons etc were confirmed as William's property in tail to his second and final son, John Montagu. William Montagu was most definitely absent, in captivity abroad, so one has to wonder if his countess would be at Wark. It is highly likely she was not. Due to the Scots campaign in the area at that time, Wark would have had a castellan, but the William Junior in le Bel's story cannot be the earl's nephew. He didn't have a nephew called William, but he did have a son, who would be around thirteen at the time. A thirteen-year-old would not be the castellan, would not lead sixty men at arms, and would not attack and kill over 200 Scots soldiers. A thirteen-year-old would most probably not sneak away in the dead of night through the enemy camp to get to the king, killing a few more Scots and their oxen on the way. Besides, the king wasn't at York, he was at a nearby manor of Cornhill.[45]

So, who was the valiant lady at Wark who was so devastatingly gorgeous and kind that she turned heads, especially that of the king? Most modern historians agree it wouldn't have been the highly noble Countess of Salisbury, not in a border castle during conflict (a conflict that wasn't resolved until a truce in May 1343[46]) whilst her husband was captured abroad and thus absent from the kingdom. Most importantly, her name was Catherine, not Alice. This valiant lady would more than likely be the wife of the castellan of the castle, who was more than capable of saving the castle and its garrison and who showed the experience of combat and military prowess.

There is another Montagu who fits perfectly and that would be Edward Montagu.[47] Edward could have easily been the castellan of Wark, a Montagu stronghold, at this time. He was in his brother William's retinue and in the service of the king's household, especially through the 1340s, and we have seen how ruthless he could be.[48] Edward Montagu was also part of the fighting force in 1341–2 to deal with this Scottish incursion. He had been summoned by writ on 4 November 1341, along with twenty-three others including his brother in law, John Segrave, and the likes of William Bohun, Earl of Northampton, and Richard, Earl of Arundel, to provide men at arms to prepare for the assault on the Scots – *De hominibus ad arma, pro expungatione Scotrum, parandis.*[49] Therefore, the noble and valiant lady would be Edward's wife, Alice – although she was only around seventeen to eighteen years old at the time – and the young William Junior would be her nephew. She was noted as his 'aunt' in le Bel's chronicle, while the actual Countess of Salisbury at the time would have been his mother. Alice could also be considered a noble lady of Salisbury due to her being married to a Montagu, as well as her own nobility; let's not forget she was a Plantagenet.

Another point of interest in favour of the lady being Alice is that Edward III is noted to have said he had not seen the noble lady since her wedding. This is perfectly feasible as Alice would have been married for only three to four years at this point and the king had been abroad most of that time. Catherine, the Countess of Salisbury, however, had been married to William Montagu for approximately thirteen years, so it's highly unlikely that Edward III hadn't seen her for all that time. As for her beauty, Alice's mother, Alice Hales, is noted as 'Alice was so beautiful as to captivate Thomas de Brotherton, Earl of Norfolk' by the antiquarian William Betham in 1801, although unfortunately he doesn't state his source.[50]

As Thomas of Brotherton married beneath him socially, and the marriage bought no financial or land gain or powerful alliance, it can be considered a love match and that his wife was a great beauty. All we really know of Alice's sister, Margaret, is how powerful she was, but their first cousin, their next nearest female blood relative, was Joan of Kent, daughter of Edmund of Woodstock, Thomas' brother, who was renowned for her beauty and intelligence, an admiration that continued for a couple of hundred years after her death.[51] Some sources say the lady in question, both at Wark and the alleged rape story, could also be Joan of Kent. William Junior of Wark, most likely the Earl of Salisbury's son, was married to Joan at this time, but whether she would be with him at Wark is debatable, and she was only thirteen. Again, William Junior may have been serving in his uncle Edward's retinue. We will see in the last chapter how the young Joan and William were most likely not living as man and wife at this stage, even though they had been married a year previous to the Wark episode.[52]

To recap, there is absolutely no reason not to give consideration that the castellan at Wark was Edward Montagu, and that his wife, Alice, was with him. Edward had the military skill, and he was playing an active role in the Scots incursion at the time Wark Castle was besieged in late 1341/early 1342. Wark Castle was a Montagu property in the thick of the Scots incursion, and as the Earl of Salisbury was unable to hold it for the king – due to being imprisoned abroad – who better to hold it for you, and your king, than your own brother, in your retinue and a professional soldier?

Edward III was young, virile, and known to enjoy the company of women, despite his famously good marriage, so if Alice was in residence at Wark, it is not beyond the realms of possibility that he found his young cousin attractive. It's here the two incidents at Wark and the subsequent attack become one. As for Packe's theory that both incidents are the reason why Alice's husband, Edward Montagu, beat her to such a degree that she eventually died, this can be dismissed when looking at the bigger picture. It is easy to speculate that if Alice of Norfolk had been the lady at Wark and object of the king's lust, that her husband could have possibly felt the need to beat her (remember, this is the fourteenth century). It is, however, highly unlikely as the Wark episode and Alice's attack were a decade apart. Ten years after the event is a long time, during which Alice spent mostly having Montagu's children. Wouldn't someone of Montagu's temper react so violently before then? If Alice was attractive and admired, she would surely have been noted in the chronicles at some point, just as her cousin Joan of Kent had been. After all, Joan married Alice's original betrothed and they were married into the same family. As mentioned previously, there are no recorded mentions of any unusual occurrences during their lengthy marriage. As Dr Ian Mortimer notes when considering Alice's situation: 'any number of other reasons could have arisen for her husband to have killed her, and the death was many years after the supposed rape. Also, it would have been difficult to hold a man guilty in law for murdering his wife when she was his chattel, even if she was the king's cousin german [first cousin]. This does not mean she was not the woman of the narrative, but the fact is incidental to the story under consideration.'[53]

Looking at the chronicles and contextual background, it is very unlikely that Edward III raped the Countess of Salisbury. It can be viewed as political propaganda due to the ongoing wars between France and England at the time. The rape story after the tournament is actually a separate issue to the incident at Wark, but they could possibly have been linked through anti-English sentiment on the Continent, to smear Edward III's name and whip up hatred for the enemy. In fact, a chronicle compiled in the early fifteenth century in the abbey of St Denis in Paris only touches on the rape and fall-out between Salisbury and his countess, and then only briefly. St Denis was the place where monks wrote about the history of French kings, and at this time of conflict between England and France many writings had an anti-English bias.[54] In addition, one has to wonder how, after the August jousting festivities, Edward III had time to travel to the castle of *Salbri* (Wark? Salisbury? Packe even mentions Bungay Castle). Also, whilst the Earl of Salisbury was due to sail overseas on 3 September 1342, he was in fact still in the country on 26 September. Edward sailed on 23 October from Portsmouth, so it is highly possible that they sailed out together as they also returned together a few months later.[55] No English chronicles or Scottish writings mention the Wark incident and surely the Scots would have jumped on any chance to defame Edward III? And although it is known that the famous chronicler Froissart (1337–1405) based his writings on le Bel's work, he could get no one to corroborate the Wark incident and there was no contemporary household rumour at the time to rely on.[56]

What can be gleaned from this contemporary account? And was it Alice of Norfolk at Wark? Jean le Bel (c.1290–1370) was born into a noble family in Hainault. He was the Canon of Liege and served in the retinue of John of Hainault, brother to the Count of Hainault, who was assisting Edward III against the Scots in 1327. Jean le Bel is known for his refusal to record anything that neither himself nor his informant had actually witnessed – he intended his narrative to be 'as close to the truth as I could, according to what I personally have seen and remembered, and also what I have heard from those who were there.'[57] He was self-effacing, intelligent, and his clear, concise writing aimed to be reliable and truthful.[58] However, not only was le Bel writing about this incident between 1352 and 1358, at least ten years or more after the flirtatious event at Wark – which must be considered a separate occurrence from the rape story – it has been considered that his retelling of stories from any oral testimony has relied too heavily on uncorroborated tales, including any bias in his witnesses. The tale of the alleged rape is one such story, possibly because it may have been popular in the current time he was writing accounts.[59]

In the words of Gransden (1976), in her excellent study on the alleged rape as a case of propaganda, 'It was better calculated to deceive because it was set in the context of well-known events and contained nothing in which was likely to appear demonstrably false to a Frenchman. In it, fact and fiction were so cleverly interwoven ... that the whole was credible.'[60]

Chapter 6

The Montagu (Monte Acuto/Montague/ Montacute) Family 1066–1400

F amously known as the Conqueror, King William I was known to have invaded England surrounded by his trusted and loyal warriors. One of his closest and loyal companions, a man who donated 120 ships for the cause of invading England and who was present at the 1066 Battle of Hastings, was his half-brother, Robert, Count of Mortain (d.1095). Despite the twelfth-century historian William of Malmsbury noting Robert was 'of a stupid and dull disposition', he was one of William I's most trusted commanders and an able military man, being sufficiently rewarded post-conquest with vast parcels of land, mainly concentrated in the south-west of England.[1]

Amongst Robert of Mortain's retinue in 1066 was a knight by the name of Drogo de Montagu, sometimes known as Dru/Drew, and we see him again the Domesday Book of 1086 as a tenant-in-chief of the king of the small settlement of Knowle Park, Wincanton, Somerset. However, he was also lord of the manor under Robert of Mortain for another twenty manors, a vast amount of land.[2]

The name Montagu, original spelling *Monte Acuto* generally means 'pointed hill', and it was unclear whether it derived from *Montaigu-les-Bois* in Normandy – where Drogo came from – or whether he took the name from the lands he was granted in Somerset. The English historian Sir Henry Churchill Maxwell-Lyte (1848–1940) was convinced it was the latter, and that is how it is on the records, although it is more than likely it was from his estates in Normandy.[3] These lands in Somerset were originally known as *Logworesbeorh/Lutgaresbury* and once belonged to the powerful eleventh-century Danish *thegn* and, therefore, aristocratic warrior Tovi the Proud who was in the retinue of King Cnut. It was at Tovi's wedding to Gytha, a daughter of the Anglo-Saxon nobleman Osgod Clapa (in a coincidental and tenuous link to Alice of Norfolk, he was a vast landowner in East Anglia) in June 1042 at Lambeth, that King Harthacanute, son of Emma of Normandy, second wife of Canute, famously died suddenly from a convulsion whilst drinking heavily.[4]

Atop the dominant hill that looked down on these lands, around the year 1035,[5] a black stone crucifix was discovered by a local blacksmith under a slab of stone, and it was considered so precious that Tovi had it moved to his hunting lodge at Waltham, Essex, where he had a church built to guard it – this church would eventually become Waltham Abbey. After Tovi's death, probably around 1043, his son lost some of his possessions, including Waltham which was then passed to Harold Godwinson by Edward the Confessor. Harold refounded the church by expanding it; the original cross found at Montacute was apparently noted for miracles and it was here he prayed for success in 1066. Whether Harold was buried here or at Bosham, if either, is disputed (another tenuous link to Alice as Bosham was her father's land).

The site where the cross was found (now known as St Michael's Hill) was given to the church and became known as Bishopston, which is how it appears in the Domesday Book of 1086. William I was more than aware of the importance and meaning of the site to the local Saxons, both religiously and politically, and thus gave it to his brother, Robert of Mortain, who, by 1068, had built a castle on top. This would have held a very significant, authoritative meaning, a reminder to the local population that they were now the submissive, conquered peoples. Not long after, there was an failed attack by the rebel forces of West Saxons, c.1068, against Montacute Castle. The rebels were either taken prisoner, killed, or executed by mutilation. The castle soon fell into disrepair and was given to Montacute Priory, together with its church, markets, and mill by Robert of Mortain's son, William, probably towards the end of eleventh century. We also see Richard Montagu, son of Drogo, granting lands to the same priory at this time. Which is just as well, as in 1106

William, Count of Mortain, lost all of his lands and property after being captured by his cousin, Henry I, at the Battle of Tinchebrai in Normandy and was imprisoned in the Tower of London.[6]

In 1148 Richard Montagu attested a charter to Queen Maud (1102–1167), also known to history as Empress Matilda. It was her second marriage to the much younger Geoffrey, Count of Anjou – also known as Plantagenet due to the sprig of the broom plant *planta gesta* he would wear in his cap – that gave rise to the Plantagenet dynasty through Matilda and Geoffrey's firstborn son, who would become Henry II and therefore the Plantagenet ancestors of Alice of Norfolk.[7]

The first notable Montagu was Simon Montagu (c.1259–1316), son and heir of the Somerset landowner William Montagu (the first of many Williams), and his wife, Bertha. On 17 March 1280 Simon, noted as the Sheriff of Somerset, and Henry de Lortyei were imprisoned for trespass of the king's forest – this would probably have been Selwood Forest, once an enormous tract of woods ranging from Dorset to Wiltshire that went across into Somerset, creating a natural barrier in Anglo-Saxon times and then known as *Sealwudu*.[8] Trespass in the king's forest was a serious offence and even had its own system of law along with border regions and maritime law.[9] Despite this, Simon went on to have an impressive military career under Edward I, including the Welsh wars of the late 1200s, as well as serving as marshal in Gascony in 1294. Two years later he bravely sailed through a line of French ships to bring much needed provisions to the besieged town of Bourg-sur-Mer. Between 1298 and his death in 1316 he served in the Scots wars, providing ships, and contributed to naval warfare. On 12 December 1299 he was created Lord Montagu, the first creation of the Montagu baronetcy. Simon was the grandfather of Edward Montagu.[10]

Simon's son and heir, William (1285–1319), 2nd Lord Montagu, married Elizabeth de Montfort (d.1354) who would eventually have custody of her son Edward and Alice of Norfolk's two youngest daughters after Alice's death in 1352.

The Montagus as the Earls of Salisbury

Edward Montagu was one of four brothers and likely the youngest sibling. William and Elizabeth Montfort had four sons – John, William, Simon and Edward – and six, possibly seven, daughters – Hawise, Elizabeth, Maud, Alice, Isabel, Mary and possibly Katherine – not necessarily in that order.

The firstborn son was John Montagu who predeceased his father in 1317. He had married Joan de Verdon (b.1303) in April 1317 at Windsor Castle, but had died shortly after, at least by 14 August 1317, and was buried in Lincoln Cathedral. Edward II seems to have been particularly upset by the death of John, the son of his favourite William, 2nd Lord Montagu, as Edward II had been extremely generous regarding young John's funeral: 'This burial appears to have been conducted with unusual ceremony. Payments were made to forty clerks saying their psalters for his soul, and to thirteen widows watching round his body; a day's provision was doled out to all the orders of Friars in Lincoln, and the King gave large alms at the divers masses celebrated in the cathedral church for the repose of the soul of the deceased, son of the Marshal of his household.'[11]

The second, but eldest surviving son was William [c.1301–1344], the son and heir after his elder brother's death in 1317, who had been a close friend and confident of Edward III for many years, with Edward III creating him 1st Earl of Salisbury in March 1337. William married Catherine Grandisson (c.1304–1349) and they had two sons and four daughters, who all made advantageous marriages. William, their firstborn son and heir (1328–1397), was the William originally betrothed to Alice of Norfolk as a child. He went on to become the 2nd Earl of Salisbury and was famous for his bigamous marriage to Alice of Norfolk's cousin, Joan of Kent, which was eventually annulled in 1349, and he was remarried to Elizabeth Mohun, daughter of Lord Mohun of Dunster. The next son, John Montagu (1330–1390), married his father's ward, Margaret Monthermer (1329–1394/95), and it was her grandfather, Ralph Monthermer (c.1270–1325), who famously married, in 1296, Edward I's daughter and Alice of Norfolk's aunt, Joan of Acre, without royal permission. Joan and her famous exploits will be discussed in the next chapter.

John and Margaret Monthermer had seven children – three sons and four daughters.[12] The firstborn son, also called John (c.1350–1400) would become the 3rd Earl of Salisbury in 1397 after the death of his uncle, the 2nd Earl. His only son and heir, Sir William, was accidentally killed in a tilting match in Windsor on 6 August 1382 by his own father, which must have been profoundly shocking for the family. Despite being married to Lady Elizabeth Fitzalan, daughter of the Earl of Arundel, the young Sir William had no issue so the title and associated lands would go to the cadet branch, that of John Montagu the Elder, and then his son, John the Younger. Incidentally, Elizabeth Fitzalan went onto have another four marriages, her second one to Thomas Mowbray whose grandmother was Margaret of Norfolk. John the Elder died in 1394/5 and his brother, the 2nd Earl, died in 1397, so the earldom inheritance went directly to John the Younger. William had not been happy about his brother and nephew inheriting due to a dispute between him and his brother, John the Elder, that had been dragging on for a few years before being settled by the John the Younger. Not before William, the 2nd Earl, had sold or left in his will everything he possibly could so his younger brother and his nephew could not inherit anything other than the earldom and associated estates.[13]

William, 1st Earl of Salisbury, and Catherine Grandisson's four daughters were Elizabeth, Philippa, Sybil and Agnes. Elizabeth (d.1359) married Giles Badlesmere (d.1338) and then married again, by April 1341, Hugh, Lord Despenser (d.1349), son of Hugh Despenser the Younger. Both these marriages had no issue and her third marriage to Guy de Bryan by 1350 produced possibly five or more children. Philippa (d.1381) married Roger Mortimer, 2nd Earl of March, grandson of the same Roger Mortimer, who was executed in 1330 after Edward III regained regal power from Mortimer and his mother, Queen Isabella. Sybil married, by 1347, Edmund Fitzalan, the disinherited eldest son of the Earl of Arundel. On 12 June 1335 Agnes married Sir John, the son and heir of Sir Roger Grey, Lord Ruthin (d.1350). At Crécy in 1346 and Calais in 1347 John Grey fought alongside his wife's uncle, Edward Montagu, as well as his brothers-in-law, William and John Montagu and Sir Walter Mauny, as well as Guy de Bryan.[14] John Grey predeceased his father shortly before 4 May 1350, and his brother Reynold (sometime Reginald) inherited the lands and title of Lord Ruthin in Wales.[15]

The second surviving son of Sir William Montagu and Elizabeth Montfort was Simon (c.1303/4–1345), born shortly after William and most likely named after his grandfather. Simon became firstly the Bishop of Worcester in 1334 and then Bishop of Ely in March 1337, around the same time as his brother, William, was elevated to the earldom of Salisbury. William and Simon would have been close in age, only two or three years apart, and by all accounts worked well together, with Simon often looking after business and family affairs for William. By 1317, aged around thirteen or fourteen, Simon was a prebendary at York Minster thanks to a royal grant, and just a year later, in November 1318, Edward II was petitioning the Pope for a dispensation for Simon to hold his own benefice, aged just fifteen. Simon was already studying at Oxford at this time.[16]

In August 1344, seven months after his brother William's death, Simon was instrumental in aiding their sister, Hawise (c1317–before 1372), and her son and daughter to have financial support, as she appeared to be estranged from her husband, a Wiltshire knight called Sir Roger Bavant (d.1355). Roger had granted all his lands to the king, including his Wiltshire estates, in August 1344 when Simon Montagu reclaimed the Wiltshire lands for his sister and her children. Hawise was still alive in 1361 when her other brother and Alice of Norfolk's husband, Edward, died. However, Hawise had died by 1372 and her only heir, her daughter Joan (her son had left to join the Franciscan Friars in Italy), wife of Sir John Dauntsey, relinquished their Wiltshire manors.[17] Interestingly, in February 1348, the Archbishop of Canterbury, along with Elizabeth Montagu and Edward Montagu, raised a complaint against Sir Roger Bavant and his accomplices for breaking onto their lands in Wiltshire and driving away twenty oxen, forty bullocks, 100 swine, 400 sheep, felling trees and crops, and carrying off said items. Six months later, in August 1348, the same complaint was bought against Sir Roger for trespass against the Archbishop of Canterbury, Elizabeth Montagu and Edward Montagu, and in October 1348 we have another complaint brought against Roger by the same Montagus for theft and trespass. A fine was paid but Roger's wife, Hawise, though still alive, wasn't mentioned, so it is likely that the only remaining Montagu brother to assist her was Edward. The Elizabeth mentioned must be their mother as their sister, also called Elizabeth, was a nun.[18]

Simon's esteemed reputation also helped another sister, Elizabeth Montagu (d.1357). Elizabeth entered Holywell Priory, Shoreditch (then in Middlesex), sometime on or just before 1334, and is described as a 'girl of noble birth' who had neither the means nor substance to support herself, and the priory could not support either Elizabeth or the other nuns in residence:

that Elizabeth de Monte Acuto , a girl of noble birth, hath entered the priory of Halywell by London as a nun; that the revenues of that house were not sufficient for the sustenance of the nuns there; that she had nothing of her own wherewith to provide for her food and clothing ,and that they out of pity for her poverty and in consideration of many benefits conferred on their house by her relations (parentes) and especially by Simon, Bishop of Worcester, had granted to her, for life, whether she should stay in the priory or be transferred to any other place and whatsoever her estate might then be, the yearly pension of 100s which the bishop used to receive from their house , to be received by her yearly on the feast of St Andrew by the hands of the keepers of the treasury of Eleanor , late queen of England ... letters of Mary, prioress of Haliwell, and the convent of that place , dated in their chapter of Haliwell , 4 November, 1334, accepting the said grant and undertaking that Elizabeth should receive the pension into her own hands and have the disposal of it.[19]

Elizabeth became prioress of Holywell Priory sometime before or around Michaelmas 1340 and gained a plenary indulgence (forgiveness of temporal/secular punishment for sins) in 1349 when the plague was raging through the country, so this would have been a way of hoping for protection from the illness. This is quite possibly when her nephew and niece, the two older children of her brother Edward and Alice of Norfolk, became victims of the plague. Simon, as Bishop of Ely, was also present with Elizabeth in April 1341 when another sister, Maud Montagu (d.1352), was consecrated as abbess of Barking Abbey, where her niece and namesake Maud, fourth child of their brother Edward and Alice of Norfolk, would also become abbess in 1377. As prioress, Elizabeth was owed £35 by a certain William Von of Staynwath in December 1354, and in July 1355 was owed £40 by Walter Bryan.[20] In January 1356 a commission of oyer and teminer was heard on complaint of Elizabeth regarding a group of men breaking the priory's 'close, houses, gates, doors and windows' to abduct Joan, daughter of John Coggeshale, the Sheriff of Essex, and marry her, as well as assaulting the priory's men and servants and stealing goods. Elizabeth's term as prioress ended on her death in c.1357.[21]

Simon appears to have been a highly regarded diocesan, thorough, diligent, and thoughtful. He considered its history of alleviating poverty when implementing important statutes to Peterhouse College, Cambridge, in 1344, which was originally a hospital for the poor, founded c.1200, and today is one of the best endowed Colleges of Cambridge University. Simon was Bishop of Ely where 'he remained until his untimely death, so it seemed to contemporaries, on 20 June 1345'. He was buried before the altar in Ely Cathedral although no trace now exists.[22]

Regarding Edward Montagu's other sisters, the eldest daughter, according to the *Complete Peerage* was Alice, who had married, by January 1332, Sir Ralph Daubney. She died sometime before July 1346 as Daubney had remarried by this point.[23] Maud was elected abbess of Barking Abbey in 1341, until her death in 1352, when another sister, Isabel, followed in her footsteps, becoming abbess from 1352 until her death in 1358.[24] We have seen that Elizabeth became the prioress of Holywell, Hawise married Sir Roger Bavant, another daughter, Katherine Montagu, married Sir William Carrington of Essex, and Mary Montagu had married Sir Richard Cogan.[25]

Around 1346–1348 Edward Montagu's mother, Elizabeth Montfort, exchanged a parcel of land to establish a chantry at St Frideswide Priory, now Christ Church Cathedral, Oxford, where her tomb can still be visited and where the land she donated to support her chantry is now part of Christ Church Meadow. The chantry was to provide a daily mass for Elizabeth's beneficiaries, both living and dead, and included herself, her parents, Sir Peter Montfort and Maud, her first husband Sir William Montagu and her second husband, Thomas, Baron Furnivall, her ten children by William, and the Bishop of Lincoln. The daughter called Katherine is not mentioned in St Frideswide Cartulary. Neither is Katherine one of the figures on her mother's tomb, which can still be seen today, albeit much damaged. In the book *Memory and the Medieval Tomb* an excellent explanation is given for Elizabeth's tomb. The figures engraved on her tomb have been identified as her children, not 'weepers' as was originally thought. Simon, as Bishop of Ely, has been identified as the figure in the central panel on the south side, whilst his sister, Maud, is in the central panel on the north side, in Benedictine dress. Within the panel on Maud's right side is another sister in Benedictine dress, who must be Isabel, and also a young boy in 'juvenile costume'. This must be Edward Montagu, confirming he must be a much younger – if not the youngest – sibling. On the left of Maud are two sisters, one in Benedictine dress, and therefore surmised to be Elizabeth, prioress of Holywell. The panel on Simon's right shows two ladies in secular dress and two men in lay attire on his left, one with a long robe, who must be his brother, William, the earl; the other lay figure would be John. That leaves three female figures, who would represent Hawise, Alice and Mary. There is no fourth figure, no Katherine, as in the St Frideswide Cartularly.[26]

Elizabeth has shown she was not only extremely devout but also her family meant a lot to her. It would have been interesting to have known

Elizabeth's reaction to her only surviving son's attack on his wife in 1351. It must have been a shock; after all, you lose your firstborn son at a young age, your second son becomes an earl and good friend of the king and your third son rises to become a bishop. Then you have Edward!

The fourth, but third surviving son and possible youngest sibling, was Edward, husband of Alice of Norfolk. His date of birth is not recorded, but on 25 April 1333 he was noted as a minor, therefore he must have been born sometime between 1313 and 1318 as his father died in 1319.[27] Edward would have come of age by March 1337 when he was knighted,[28] and his year of birth is often dated c.1315/16.[29] We can narrow it down to the point that Edward was approximately eight or nine years older than Alice, who we know was married to him by the time she was aged fourteen, as per her father's Inquisition Post Mortem.[30] As previously mentioned, Edward Montagu was a landless younger son from a cadet branch within a powerful family of the time, who married an earl's daughter, Edward III's first cousin, due to his elder brother William's friendship and connection with the king and Thomas of Brotherton astutely linking with Edward III's new men. Edward Montagu most likely did not remember his father, as he would have been extremely young at the time of his father's death, and there was quite an age gap between him and his two older brothers, although he did have a stepfather from an early age. Edward's mother, Elizabeth, remarried when Edward was approximately six years old, to Sir Thomas Furnivall on the 8 June 1322, for which Sir Thomas was pardoned and fined for marrying her without royal licence.[31] There was no issue from this second marriage.

It is interesting to note that Edward's lawlessness became prominent after the deaths of his two older brothers – William in January 1344 and Simon in June 1345 – showing they most likely had a controlling influence over him. We saw how William had a hand in the arrangements of the marriages of Edward and Alice's children, for example.

Edward Montagu married again after Alice's death in 1352, although the only information regarding the woman who married Edward is her name, Joan. He had two children that we know of by Joan: a son, another Edward, born c. June 1361; and another daughter called Audrey, but known as Etheldreda, the same as his first daughter with Alice. It appears to be an unusual name; St Etheldreda (c.636–c.679) was one of four daughters of a king of East Anglia in the seventh century, who, despite being married twice, remained a virgin and founded the original monastery on her dower lands of the Isle of Ely, where Ely cathedral now stands. Her feast day is 23 June so may have had some meaning for Edward.[32]

Being only seven weeks old when his father died, and in the wardship of the king, the baby Edward sadly died a couple of months after his father in October 1361, leaving his sister Etheldreda, aged approximately two years old, as the heir. This means that the daughter Elizabeth, who is noted as marrying Sir John Braose of Tetbury (son of sir Thomas Braose and Beatrice Mortimer, the widow of the young Edward of Norfolk, Alice's brother) in January 1360/61 would have died by the time her father died as she is not mentioned in the Inquisitions Post Mortem of her father or baby half-brother.[33] Edward Montagu died in July 1361, most likely at Bungay as he was there in January when arranging his daughter Elizabeth's marriage to Sir John Braose. However, he was still being summoned to Parliament as late as March 1361.[34]

Edward Montagu's lineage appears to last longer than Alice's did. In 1374 Etheldreda and her mother, Joan, are being sued for the manor of Redenhall by Philip de Aylesbury and Richard de Montfort, who had married Agnes and Roes [Rose] Branteston respectively, a family who had held Redenhall in Norfolk up to the year 1300. Etheldreda is noted on this claim as the 'daughter and heiress of Edward de Montagu', but the petition was postponed 'owing to her being under age'.[35] If she was two years old when her father died in 1361, this would make her fifteen at this time. The petition is bought again in 1379, the only difference being that Richard de Monfort is absent, so he must have died, and the order is aimed at Sir Hugh de Strauleye, also known as Strelley/Stranley (b.c1352–1390), who is now the husband of Etheldreda, as well as her mother, Joan, the widow of Edward Montagu. So, Joan is still alive in 1379 and Etheldreda is married with a son, and she is probably aged around twenty at this time. Hugh and Etheldreda went on to have two sons, the son and heir being Sir John Strauleye (b.c 1378) and a second son, Sir Hugh Strauleye. Hugh Strauleye the Elder died by either March or August 1390, with his son, John, aged eleven, named as heir.[36] Of these two grandsons of Edward Montagu, Sir John married a lady called Joan by 1408 and had died by 1428.[37] Sir Hugh, who served at Agincourt in 1415, married Joyce Wykes and was still alive in 1424, and their son, also John, was married to Elizabeth, who, in 1471, was petitioning the king and council regarding the Strelley manor of Hazelbadge.[38] There is a probable son of John and Elizabeth, named Robert, living in the reign of Edward IV, so Edward Montagu's lineage by his second marriage lasted at least one hundred years after his death in 1361.

A great-niece of Edward Montagu and a younger sister of John Montagu, the 3rd Earl of Salisbury, was a lady called Katherine. In 1376 a certain Katherine Montagu broke her vows and deserted Bungay Priory, and in 1846 the Suffolk historian and clergyman Alfred Suckling (1796–1856) assumed a connection between her and Edward Montagu. An order was given out to arrest and deliver Katherine back to the prioress of Bungay as she was 'vagabond in secular attire in divers parts of the realm', and a danger to her soul. Unusually, this was a petition by the bishop of the diocese of Norwich, Henry Despencer, whose grandfather was the famous favourite of Edward II, Hugh Despencer the Younger. Petitions for arrests of wayward monks and nuns were usually the courtesy of the abbess or prior, but Henry of Norwich had written letters on the matter of Katherine Montagu to Edward III who issued the petition, which could mean that this was indeed the sister of the 3rd Earl of Salisbury. Perhaps she didn't want a life of abstinence. Many women and girls were admitted to convents against their will and for many it was not a vocation. Younger daughters especially could be assigned to the ecclesiastical way of life for a myriad of reasons; for example, their families couldn't afford to marry them off, or they were considered 'insane'. Many, though, did end up returning to their monastery or priory; the threat of excommunication and bringing shame upon one's family was a very difficult situation to stand up against as a medieval woman. However, in 1380 a Katherine Montagu is listed as the abbess of Bungay.[39]

John, the 3rd Earl of Salisbury, also had two other sisters who had dedicated themselves to serving God: Sybil Montagu (1368–1420), who became Abbess of Amesbury Priory, and Margaret, a nun in Barking Abbey. John's brother Thomas Montagu became the dean of Salisbury from 1382 to 1404, and another sister, Eleanor (d.before November 1396) married a Devonshire knight.[40]

John Montagu, 3rd Earl of Salisbury and last Montagu of the fourteenth century, was a loyal supporter of Richard II, even after Richard was usurped by the new king, Henry IV. John Montagu, along with John Holland, third son of Joan of Kent and Thomas Holland, John Holland's nephew, took part in a rebellion against the new king and aimed to reinstate Richard II upon the throne. This became known as the Epiphany Rising and was highly unsuccessful, leading to the execution of all three in early January 1400. John Montagu's son Thomas Montagu (1388–1428) had estates restored to him in June 1409. He was summoned to Parliament as the Earl of Salisbury in October 1409 and had his father's titles and estates fully restored to him in 1421.[41]

Chapter 7

Plantagenet Women

Alice's first cousin, Joan of Kent (September 1326/7–August 1385)

During their childhood, Alice and her sister Margaret's nearest female blood relative was their first cousin, Joan of Kent. Joan was the daughter of Alice's uncle, Edmund of Woodstock, Earl of Kent, her father's full-blood younger brother. It is possible that Alice's youngest daughter was named Joan after her aunt, Joan of Kent.

There is much written about Joan, including the tale of her being the catalyst for the Order of the Garter story, much dismissed by modern historians and most likely a fanciful tale with no substance as the story didn't appear until much later in a fifteenth-century chronicle.[1] However, to keep the links with the Norfolk Plantagenets, the Order of the Garter story won't be dwelt on here. Joan achieved notoriety during her lifetime due to her bigamous marriages, and third and final marriage to Edward the Black Prince. Due to the latter's early death, his son by Joan became Richard II after the death of his grandfather, Edward III. Much like her cousin Margaret of Norfolk, Alice's sister, Joan has many historiographies worthy of any blockbuster film.

Joan of Kent's mother was Margaret Wake, daughter of John, Lord Wake, and Margaret was first cousin to Roger Mortimer, 1st Earl of March, through their mothers, the Fienne sisters, Joan and Margaret. Margaret was the widow of John Comyn, who was killed at the Battle of Bannockburn in June 1314, and their young son had died in his infancy. She married for the second time to Edmund of Woodstock in December 1325.[2] Five years later, her cousin Roger Mortimer would be the one to order the execution of Margaret's second husband and Joan's father, Edmund, Earl of Kent, in 1330.

Margaret and Edmund had four children in the space of four years, namely Edmund, Joan, Margaret and John, though not necessarily in that birth order. The only one with a certain birthdate is the youngest sibling, John, as we know he was the posthumous child, born 7 April 1330, a couple of weeks after his father's execution on 19 March 1330. Young Edmund was the eldest son and heir, although not necessarily the eldest child, but had died a minor in the king's ward sometime by October 1331, with his younger brother John being named as his heir.[3]

Joan of Kent's birth date is often given as September 1328, though the historian Kathryn Warner has challenged this more thoroughly, and it does indeed seem more likely Joan was born in September 1326 or 1327. After her childless brother John's early death, aged just twenty-two, in 1352, his Inquisition Post Mortem names Joan as his heir. Only two county jurors give an exact date for Joan's birth, being aged twenty-five or more on 29 September, or aged twenty-six or more,[4] giving a birth year of either 1326 or 1327. As Joan and her brother Edmund are noted as lifting their baby brother, John, from the font in 1330 – 'Edmund, son of the said Edmund, late Earl of Kent and brother John de Grenstede, prior of the order of Friars Preachers of Arundell and Joan, sister of the said Edmund, son of Edmund, lifted the said John from the sacred font on Tuesday 7 April' – it seems Joan must have been more than eighteen months old (if her usual given birth date is 1328) to have this responsibility and capability. It is highly likely she was aged nearer four years old at this time.[5]

There is a second daughter of whom little is known, Margaret of Kent. Her betrothal was arranged by Edward III on 4 April 1340, whereby Margaret was betrothed to Amaniu Albret, the firstborn son of the lord of Albret, Bernat-Etz V, as part of a powerful treaty in Gascony: '4 April 1340. London. For treating upon the betrothal. Assignment of Oliver de Ingham, seneschal of Gascony , and Antonio Usodimare, lieutenant of the constable of Bordeaux , to treat and agree with Bernat-Etz [V], lord of Albret upon the betrothal and marriage of Amaniu, his firstborn son and Margaret, daughter of Edmund [of Woodstock], late Earl of Kent, the king's uncle , and upon the settling of the dower, marriage portion and gift on account of the marriage and for strengthening the security for the same and doing all other things necessary for the same, the king promising to confirm Ingham and Usodimare's actions.'[6] Oliver Ingham, Edward III's trusted seneschal of Gascony, was tasked with Antony Usumaris, lieutenant of the constable of Bordeaux, to 'treat for a marriage between Amanenus, eldest son of Bernardet lord de la Bret and Margaret, daughter of the late earl of Kent'.[7]

Both the Gascony Rolls and a genealogy of the Albrets gives a birth date c.1327 for Margaret, with her death c.1352. Margaret of Kent had most definitely predeceased her brother John by his death in December 1352 as his Inquistion Post Mortem names Joan as his only heir, meaning he also had no issue despite having been married in 1348 to Elizabeth, the daughter of Joanna of Hainault, younger sister to Queen Philippa.[8]

Knowing Edmund of Woodstock married Margaret Wake in December 1325, and if we use the Albret Genealogy to estimate Margaret's birth date as around 1327 (the Albret genealogy doesn't cite any references other than the Gascony Rolls unfortunately), Joan must have been born late 1326 or early 1327 as it would be possible to have two babies in the same year, though highly unlikely given that a woman had to be churched for six weeks before her husband could come anywhere near her; 1328 could also be Margaret's birth year as her betrothal of marriage is given as 1340, when she would have reached the legal age of twelve. As Edmund, the heir, and Joan were old enough to lift their baby brother, John, from the font in 1330, and Margaret isn't mentioned, it is highly likely that Joan was the elder sister and possibly eldest child. Of course, amongst all this conjecture, they could have been twins. After all, Queen Philippa, cousin-by-marriage, and future guardian and mother-in-law of Joan of Kent, was pregnant aged twenty-three, twenty-four, twenty-six, twenty-seven and twenty-eight, with her seventh child being born a mere thirteen months after her sixth.[9] Whatever the chronology of the Kent children, Margaret Wake and Edmund of Woodstock were fertile enough to have a baby every year from 1326 to 1330 and Joan would have been close in age to her cousin, Alice of Norfolk.

Margaret Wake was, in her own right, the heir to her brother, Thomas Wake (c.1298–1349) who, despite being married to Blanche of Lancaster, eldest daughter of Edward II's cousin, Henry of Lancaster, for thirty-three years, died childless in May1349. Margaret followed him to the grave a mere four months later,[10] probably from the plague. Joan of Kent's brother Edmund had died young a few years previously, most definitely by October 1331,[11] so her younger brother, John, became heir, not only to the earldom of Kent but also to his mother's and the Wakes' landed fortunes. John had married a niece of Queen Philippa but died without issue and thus Joan of Kent became the heiress to a fortune in 1352.[12]

After the political fall-out after the execution of the Earl of Kent in March 1330, Margaret Wake must have feared for her safety and that of her children. Her brother, Thomas Wake, had fled abroad, and as we have seen, he had been implicated in the plan to rescue Edward II along with Edmund: 'Thomas Wake of Lydel, who, having been cited of adherence to Edmund, earl of Kent, who was adjudged to death for sedition in the Parliament summoned at Winchester, has secretly withdrawn from the realm.'[13] Margaret's brother-in-law, Thomas of Brotherton, also went abroad to Gascony soon after, despite not being implicated at all in the plot, probably thanks to his son's marriage to Roger Mortimer's daughter. On the day of the arrest of Edmund, 14 March 1330, orders were given in the king's name to two of the king's yeomen, John Payn and Nicholas de Langeford, to escort Margaret, Countess of Kent, and her children from Arundel Castle to the custody of the sheriff at Salisbury Castle until further notice, being allowed only two female servants to accompany her. The king's clerks, William de Holyns and Roger atte Ashe, were to confiscate all of Margaret's jewellery and goods and Roger was given custody of Arundel Castle.[14] Her advanced stage of pregnancy must have rendered this trip impossible and on 20 March 1330 she was granted a mark (13s 4d) a day expenses for herself and her children. Margaret and her small children were guarded, and it was at Arundel Castle that she was informed of the fate of her husband,

and of where Edmund's posthumous son, John, was born a couple of weeks later.[15]

When Edward III overthrew his mother, Queen Isabella, and Roger Mortimer's regime in the Nottingham coup of November 1330 he moved quickly to restore all those who had been attainted by the judicial murder of his uncle, Edmund of Woodstock. Edmund's widow and family were restored, and Margaret's brother, Thomas Wake, was forgiven, lands restored, and safe passage and protection given to travel back to England.[16] Margaret and her family were taken under the royal wing, with Joan being a favourite of Queen Philippa who was known for her kindness and empathy.[17] The execution of Edmund, who had escorted Phillipa with his brother Thomas to her coronation back in February 1330, must have shocked the queen as much as anyone, but Margaret's children were safe and Edmund and John were now valuable wards of the king. In March 1331 a writ was issued in favour of Margaret having custody of the lands during the minority of Edmund, son and heir of Edmund, late Earl of Kent. In April 1331 the king is noted as presenting a church in Lincoln 'as it is the king's gift by reason of his custody of the lands and heir of Edmund, late earl of Kent, tenant in chief', and we know Edmund, the young son and heir, had died by October as on 16 October 1331 a grant was made to William Bohun regarding a manor that was 'now in the king's hands by reason of his custody of John, son and heir of Edmund, late earl of Kent'.[18]

Joan of Kent had three marriages in all, the first one in Spring 1340 to Thomas Holland (b.c.1314), the second son of Sir Robert Holland, a knight in Lancashire, and himself a knight of the royal household. Thomas was about twenty-six years old at the time, whilst Joan was thirteen to fourteen years old (not necessarily twelve, as explained above regarding her brother John's Inquisition Post Mortem), and some sources say that because he was much older he bullied and cajoled her into the marriage. It could just as easily have been a love match as he was still a landless knight at this point, and there was no sign Joan would become the great heiress she would in 1352, as her brother John was still alive at this time. Besides, Joan and Thomas would go on to have five children together and when she died, Joan requested to be buried beside Thomas, not her third and final husband, the Black Prince.

Thomas Holland was soon abroad after his clandestine marriage to the young Joan, leaving for Prussia later that year, and continued to make his fortune as a soldier, becoming a very able military commander, distinguishing himself in 1343 with the Earl of Derby's entourage, and earning his fortune at Crécy alongside Joan's sixteen-year-old brother, John, Earl of Kent, and in the retinue of the Black Prince – who would be Joan of Kent's third husband – in 1346.[19]

Whilst Holland was away, negotiations began for Joan's marriage in 1340 to the son and heir of the Earl of Salisbury, the thirteen-year-old William (original betrothed to Alice of Norfolk, who was married to his uncle Edward by this time). The Earl of Salisbury was nothing if not ambitious and although Joan was not an heiress, unlike the other Montagu betrothals, she was royal, a granddaughter of Edward I and cousin to the king. We have seen how this son and heir was originally betrothed to Alice of Norfolk as a five-year-old, and one reason she may have ended up marrying the earl's brother instead of his son may be down to the death of her own brother, therefore making Alice and her sister, Margaret, extremely valuable heiresses, although Margaret was already married. What could be better than marrying your wayward younger brother into royalty as well as your son?[20]

The Earl of Salisbury had been captured by the French in April 1340 and released on parole in September 1340, although his exact date of returning to England is unknown.[21] Salisbury must have been straight onto the marriage arrangements for his son and heir on his return to England; whether the Montagus knew of Joan's clandestine marriage to Holland or not, or if they were confident they could pay him off, for example, Joan and William Junior were married by February 1341.[22] Their marriage would be annulled in November 1349, and during that time it's nice to think Alice and Joan would have been companions, or at least met at some point, especially as Joan was officially Countess of Salisbury from 1344 to 1349. Alice spent the 1340s having children and that decade saw Joan become the wife of Alice's nephew.

Thomas Holland began petitioning for Joan to be returned as his wife in the autumn of 1347, after he had earned a fortune in June 1347 from Edward III for ransoming a military prisoner. This could indicate why it took so long for him to bring the petition against Joan's marriage to William Montagu. Thomas declared that their own wedding had been witnessed and consummated, which Joan supported in her later testimony, stating she had only agreed to the Montagu marriage after great pressure from family and friends.[23] Interestingly, William, who was now the 2nd Earl of Salisbury, seems to have made sure that Joan was, for all intents and purposes, cut-off from communicating with anyone other than himself, and most likely, her own family, who were all complicit in supporting her marriage to the earl and not to Thomas. William's grandmother, Lady Elizabeth Montagu, Dowager Countess of Salisbury, the same lady who would have custody of Alice of Norfolk's daughters, was also 'going beyond the seas on the king's service by his command,'[24] and although it is not known why, it is generally thought this was to intervene with the papal court in Avignon regarding her grandson's marriage to Joan. In May 1348 the Pope issued a mandate to the bishops of London and Norwich, and the Archbishop of Canterbury:

> Mandate, on petition of Thomas de Holand, knight, stating that his wife Joan, daughter of Edmund, earl of Kent, to whom he was married upwards of eight years ago, was given in marriage to William, son of William de Monteacuto, during the absence from the realm of Thomas, then in Prussia, and that the said William and Margaret, Joan's mother, opposed Thomas in recovering his conjugal rights. The cause was, at the instance of Thomas, brought before the pope, and a suit of nullity of marriage against William and Margaret and Joan was ordered to be heard by Aymar, cardinal of St. Anastasia's, but Joan was caused by William to be detained in England, and kept in custody. She is to be enlarged so as to be able to appoint a proctor, and carry on the cause.[25]

After various delaying tactics by the Earl of Salisbury and Joan's mother, in the summer of 1349 Joan finally had her own magistrate and a papal bull was declared in November 1349 that she was to be returned to her legal husband, Thomas Holland, and that they were wed in the eyes of the church. Their first child, a son and heir called Thomas, arrived just a year later.[26]

It is interesting to note that Joan had no children by Montagu, and although consummation of a marriage could be delayed when the children married young, Joan and William were man and wife for eight years and both went on to have children in further marriages. It appears that as soon as the Pope ruled in favour of Joan and Holland in November 1349, William Montagu married again with almost immediate effect at the end of 1349, to Elizabeth Mohun, one of three daughters, heiresses of Lord John Mohun of Dunster, Somerset. As noted in her thesis on Joan of Kent, Lawne states these are both indicators that the Montagus knew of the Holland marriage from the beginning and had taken steps to ensure a Plan B – no heirs by Joan and another marriage (that possibly took a few months beforehand to arrange) lined up. All concerned parties moved forward with life, and as Lawne states, 'there is no evidence of any ill feeling subsequently between William, Joan and Thomas'.[27]

Joan went on to have five children in all with Thomas, three sons and two daughters, with the firstborn son and heir, Thomas, being conceived almost immediately. Edmund Holland died as an infant and John Holland would become the eventual Duke of Exeter in 1397. Their two daughters, Joan and Maud (also known as Matilda), married well, with Maud becoming the second wife of Sir Hugh de Courtney, whose first wife had been Margaret de Bryan, only daughter of Edward Montagu's niece, Elizabeth Montagu, and Guy de Bryan. Thomas Holland rose through the military ranks of Edward III's reign and in 1359 became the king's captain and lieutenant in France and Normandy. He died in Rouen on 26/28 December 1360. The widowed Joan would be married again within the year. By spring 1361 the son and heir of Edward III, Lord Edward, also known as the Black Prince, and childhood friend of Joan, declared his love for her. On 7 September 1361 a papal bull of dispensation was issued (as they were related within the third degree of consanguinity as cousins) and on 18 October 1361 a declaration by the Archbishop of Canterbury confirmed that the marriage at Windsor of 'the prince of Wales with the countess of Kent' had occurred a week previously, on 10 October 1361.[28] The Chandos Herald, in the employ of Sir John Chandos, constable of Aquitaine, close friend and military comrade of the Black Prince, who had fought alongside him at Crécy, wrote of Joan that 'the noble Prince married a lady of great worth, who had won his affection, and was lovely, agreeable and wise.'[29]

Although Edward III had been in the process of marriage negotiations between his son Edward and Margaret of Flanders when Prince Edward took it upon himself to marry Joan without permission, or notifying his father, the Black Prince's marriage to Joan of Kent was supported by the king and queen. The Black Prince and Joan moved their entire household to Bordeaux when Edward III gave his son the duchy of Aquitaine, and Joan went on to have two sons by him; Edward was born in 1365 and a brother, Richard, was born in 1367. Young Edward died in 1370/71 of plague and in 1371 the family returned to England with the Black Prince in poor health. He died in 1376, predeceasing his father, Edward III. His surviving son, Richard, would become Richard II after the death of his grandfather, Edward III, in 1377. Joan remained popular with both the nobility and common people, and according to her entry in the Oxford Dictionary of National Biography, she became very overweight in her last few years due to illness, dying at Wallingford Castle in August 1385. She chose to be interred next to Thomas Holland at Greyfriars in Stamford, Lincolnshire, not with the Black Prince in Canterbury (who had had a chantry chapel and ceiling boss of her face made for her).

Joan's beauty, life story and history have survived through time, described by Froissart as 'the most beautiful and loving woman in all of England'.[30]

Mary of Woodstock, Nun-Princess

Mary (March 1279–May 1332) was the sixth daughter of Edward I and Eleanor of Castile, one of the older half-sisters of Thomas of Brotherton and, therefore, Alice of Norfolk's aunt. In 1285, when Mary was six years old, her grandmother, Edward I's mother, Eleanor of Provence, planned to retire to Amesbury Priory and she requested two of her granddaughters to accompany her. One was Mary and the other was Mary's cousin, Eleanor of Brittany, daughter of Edward I's sister, Beatrice. Mary's mother, Queen Eleanor, seemed more reluctant about her daughter taking the veil – maybe she thought Mary was not cut out for the priory life or that Mary was too young to understand what she would be giving up – although talks of her entering the nunnery had been discussed between the Abbess of Fontevraud and Edward I since 1282.[1]

In November 1284 a letter from the Abbess of Fontevraud made its way to Queen Eleanor, possibly to placate and soften Eleanor's doubts of Mary entering Amesbury at such a young age. The letter addresses the queen as her 'most excellent and beloved lady', and says what a major honour it would be for her daughter, of royal blood, to decorate the religious order, ending the letter by calling Eleanor the 'most excellent mother'.[2] It seems Eleanor was not quite placated, and the contemporary chronicler and Dominican Friar of London Nicholas Trevet (c.1257/65–c.1334) wrote in his chronicle *Annales Sex Regum Angliae* that in 1285 'Mary, the daughter of the king of England, becomes a nun at Ambresberia, with the consent of her parents, although with difficulty, at the request of the king's mother.'

Edward I had eventually agreed with his mother, Eleanor of Provence, and in August 1285, aged only six years old, Mary, along with thirteen other noble young ladies, took the pledge to serve Christ, with her official veiling as a nun in 1291, aged twelve. Mary was unique in the fact that not only was she unusually young to enter life as a nun, she was the first member of the royal family to do so in one hundred years.[3] However, with an annual allowance of £100 (approximately £70,000 today) rising to £200 after the death of her grandmother, Mary of Woodstock was to be no ordinary nun.

Monasteries and nunneries were around a long time before the Norman invasion of England, with places such as Glastonbury and Worcester, for example, being sacrosanct, and Amesbury was no exception.[4] Believed to be the site of pagan worship, a monastery was founded here in c.979 by Queen Alfrida (c.945–c.1000–1002), second wife of King Edgar of England (c.942–975). Alfrida also founded Wherwell Abbey in Hampshire c.986, where she retired to as a nun and where she was most likely buried. In 1177 Henry II dissolved Alfrida's foundation and by a papal bull he refounded Amesbury as a house of the Order of Fontevraud in Anjou, France. The Plantagenets were great benefactors of Fontevraud, with Henry II's widow Eleanor of Aquitaine taking up residence there. Amesbury would be a royal favourite for the future generations.[5]

Mary's grandmother, Eleanor of Provence, had been planning on entering Amesbury Priory during her widowhood and spared no expense in preparing and bestowing improvements upon it for her arrival. In 1280 the keeper of Chute Forest was ordered to supply 'ten oaks fit for timber for certain works that Queen Eleanor, the king's mother, is causing to be made at Amesbury'. The bailiff of Clarendon was also ordered to supply twenty oaks from Buckholt forest for the same works.[6] In July 1281 another fifteen oaks from Chute Forest and twelve oaks from Melksham Forest were ordered to supply Amesbury Priory for Eleanor's works.[7] What these works were that needed so many oaks is anyone's guess, but it was most likely new living quarters for herself and her granddaughters.

Amesbury had been lavishly and expansively restored in the late 1170s through to the early 1180s by Henry II, and consisted of the usual cloisters as well as a 200-ft dormitory, large dining hall and kitchen, a main hall, a buttery, pantry, and suites of rooms for the prioress. It also had an infirmary, stables, barns, herb gardens, fishponds and a gatehouse.[8] Eleanor of Provence entered Amesbury a few months after Mary, in July 1286, died there in June 1291, and was buried there in

September 1291. Her tomb, like many other medieval burials, is now, unfortunately, lost.[9]

Despite Amesbury being a Benedictine House, an order that usually attracted wealthy and powerful benefactors and patrons, Mary of Woodstock appears to have found the monastic life neither vocational nor career guided, and most definitely did not join to avoid marriage, as many noble women did. Once final vows had been taken – in Mary's case when she was twelve – one was expected to be bound to their particular abbey for life.[10] Mary, however, enjoyed an inordinate amount of freedom and leisure, no doubt related to her exalted position as daughter of Edward I. Shortly after entering Amesbury in August 1285, by the autumn Mary was back at the royal court with family at Winchester and spent much of the following spring in 1286 with her family before her parents set off to France, returning in 1289 when she, along with her sisters and her young brother, Edward, were at Dover to welcome their parents' return. Mary was often at court, including at the wedding of her sister, Joan of Acre, in 1290, as well as receiving family, and there were frequent visits made to Amesbury by Edward I. Mary was a keen patron of literacy, having been given a writing tablet when she was young by her mother. Mary's mother, Queen Eleanor, had long sponsored the production of her own texts, having her own *scriptorium*, and this love of literacy appears to have continued with Mary. She became a patron of Nicholas Trevet, commissioning her own chronicle, and continued the extensive patronage of Plantagenet women in promoting their lineage, historiography, and their place in medieval society.[11]

However, Mary also found it difficult to live within her means. She had a penchant for gambling, and amassed large debts, despite her generous allowance, yet again proving how unsuited she was to the life of a nun. Edward I paid off her debts on numerous occasions. In January 1302 the Sheriff of Southampton was to make sure Mary continued to receive twenty tuns of wine per annum, which she had been used to receiving. Later that year, in August, Mary was to receive forty old oaks per year for her hearth, compensation of £200 per annum for 'maintenance of her chamber at Amesbury', as well as various manors across Wiltshire, Somerset and on the Isle of Wight. In March 1305 she received the custody and wardship during the minority of the heir of William de Pageham, and a month later received all the escheats (reversion of property to the Crown in the event of no heirs), wards, marriages and knights' fees of the manors that had been awarded to her in 1302.[12] That is a lot of wealth.

As mentioned in an earlier chapter, Mary of Woodstock was the most frequent visitor to the royal household of her younger brothers, Thomas of Brotherton and Edmund of Woodstock. The household accounts show that between 27 June and 4 October 1305 Mary visited her brothers eleven times, staying a total of up to five days on each visit.[13] What may explain the frequency is that during the summer of 1305 the boys were staying at Ludgershall Castle, Wiltshire, not far from Amesbury Priory, under the guardianship of Mary. Ludgershall was a comfortable, fortified royal residence that Henry III, Thomas of Brotherton's paternal grandfather, had turned into a comfortable hunting lodge.[14] This was not unusual for Mary as she often had guardianship over her sister Joan of Acre's daughters at Amesbury, and she had remained close to her stepmother, Queen Marguerite, since her presence had been requested by her father to attend the queen at Woodstock in 1301 for the birth of Edmund, Thomas' younger brother.[15]

Mary was given manors during the minority of her nephew, the young heir Gilbert de Clare, after the death of his mother, Mary's sister, Joan of Acre, in April 1307. Mary was still with Queen Marguerite at Northampton Castle in June 1307, along with Thomas and Edmund, when news of her father's illness reached them. Despite a pilgrimage to Canterbury and Dover by all four of them, news that Edward I had died reached them on their return journey. Queen Marguerite quickly sent Thomas and Edmund back to Northampton Castle while she followed more slowly, and Mary returned to Amesbury Priory.[16]

Mary had not been a conventional nun, but it had served her well. Entrusted with the care of her own nieces and nephews over the years, she still enjoyed the good life and obviously had a bit of a gambling addiction. She seems to have remained close to her family members, developing a solid relationship with her stepmother, Queen Marguerite, as well as her brother, Edward II, during his turbulent years with their father by offering him a refuge to stay. Mary was, as mentioned previously, the patron of the chronicler Nicholas Trevet (also spelt Trevit), commissioning him and showing she had inherited her mother and grandmother's love of the *scriptorium*. These Plantagenet women were strong patrons of the arts, scribing their history, which has come down to us in time.[17]

It is highly possible that Mary of Woodstock would have met a young Alice of Norfolk, her niece. Alice would have been around eight years old when Mary died on 29 May 1332. Mary was buried at Amesbury, joining her young half-sister, Eleanor, younger sister of Thomas and Edmund, who was also buried at Amesbury in 1311, aged six years.[18]

'She was interred in the monastery which for forty-eight years had been her principal abode. The hand of Time has been heavy upon this structure, and a picturesque ruin, with its mantle of ivy and wreath of wild flowers, is all that now remains to point out the spot which was at once the abode and the tomb of the nun princess.'[19]

Joan of Acre (1272–1307)

Joan was the second surviving daughter of Edward I and his queen, Eleanor of Castile (1241–1290), born before her father became king and whilst her parents were in Acre, in Palestine, on the Ninth Crusade, hence the reason she is known as Joan of Acre. Although her younger half-brother, Thomas of Brotherton, was only seven when she died – and therefore Alice of Norfolk would never have known her aunt – there are a few connections via marriage to the Norfolk Plantagenets. Joan was also known for marrying for love, without her father's permission. In fact, Joan had a history of being fearless where her father was concerned – she may have had the Plantagenet blood but she was also reputed to have the fiery temperament of her mother. Known as spirited, self-willed and determined, not only did Joan openly support her younger brother, the future Edward II, when he was cut off and banished to

Windsor castle by their father in 1305, she was rather good at running up debts, similar to her sister Mary of Woodstock, that Edward I paid off.[8]

Joan spent her formative years in the care of her grandmother in Ponthieu and returned home to England in 1278 after her father had arranged her marriage to Hartman, son of the king of Romans. The marriage was delayed (possibly because the six-year-old Joan was delayed in returning to England), and Hartman died in a boating accident in December 1281.[1] Edward I soon arranged for another betrothal, and on 30 April 1290 the eighteen-year-old Joan was married in Westminster to the forty-six-year-old Gilbert de Clare, Earl of Hereford and Gloucester, one of the most powerful Marcher lords of the day.

Between 1291 and 1295 Joan and Gilbert had four children. The eldest was Gilbert de Clare (1291–1314), son and heir, as well as being Edward I's eldest grandchild. He married Matilda (also known as Maud), daughter of Richard de Burgh, Earl of Ulster, at Westminster in September 1308. Joan was to place Gilbert de Clare, aged ten years old, in the household of Queen Marguerite at the order of Edward I. Gilbert would therefore have been familiar with his young cousins, Thomas of Brotherton and Edmund of Woodstock.[2] Gilbert – known as 'the Red' – was killed at the Battle of Bannockburn in June 1314, the only high-ranking earl to be killed that day amongst the heavy English losses. He had, allegedly, rushed into battle 'seeking to carry off the glory of the first clash', without his coat of arms, otherwise he would most likely have been taken prisoner instead of succumbing to the attacking Scots.[3]

Joan of Acre's next child, and eldest daughter, was Eleanor de Clare (1292–1337) who married Hugh Despenser the Younger in 1306. He would become the second favourite of her uncle, Edward II, and assist in his downfall. When Hugh was executed in 1326, Eleanor married Sir William la Zouche. The third child, a second daughter, Margaret de Clare (c.1293/94–1342), married Piers Gaveston in 1307, aged thirteen or fourteen, and after his execution in 1312 married Hugh Audley, now the Earl of Gloucester. The fourth and last child was Elizabeth (1295–1360). She married John de Burgh, son and heir of the Earl of Ulster and brother of Matilda, her brother's wife. Elizabeth and John were married a day after Gilbert and Matilda, in September 1308. Elizabeth was a fine example of how a medieval noblewoman was used within political power. By the time she was twenty-seven she had been married and widowed three times to her uncle Edward II's favourites, but did manage to live a long and peaceful widowhood, as well as being the founder of Clare College, Cambridge.[4]

Elizabeth was born in the September, just three months before the death of Her father, Gilbert, on 7 December 1295. Gilbert died suddenly and unexpectedly at Monmouth Castle, the recently renovated and fortified residence of Edward I's younger brother, Edmund Crouchback. Joan oversaw the removal of her husband's body from Monmouth to Tewkesbury Abbey where he was laid to rest next to his father and ancestors at the high altar.[5] Widowed aged just twenty-three, Joan of Acre was now a very wealthy and landed noblewoman, and in January 1296 she paid homage for her lands to her father the king, Edward I. He restored those lands that she had held jointly with Gilbert, but it is possible Joan had concerns regarding the safety of her very young children; Gilbert was only four years old at the death of his father and now the heir to a vast fortune. It was agreed all four would stay and have their own household within the walled safety of Bristol Castle, and at the end of January 1296 Edward I ordered the constable of the castle, Nicholas Frembaud, to take the children into the king's houses – except the tower – along with the people Joan would appoint for their custody. Bristol Castle was a strong fortress with noble housing within. It was Edward I's headquarters for his English estates and housed the country's exchequer.[6]

One of the requests from Edward I to Joan after paying homage was the promise not to remarry without the king's consent. After all, anyone marrying Joan would then have access to her vast wealth and estates and could be seen as a threat to Edward. Joan may have had unusual freedom as a Marcher lord in her own right, but a choice of husband was not an option and Edward I wasted no time in finding a new suitor for his wilful daughter. He chose Amadeus V, Count of Savoy, with a betrothal date of March 1297. It was a marriage Joan of Acre had no intention of partaking in.[7]

Many of Gilbert de Clare's household familia stayed with Joan when she became their lord. One of these was a young squire of unknown origin named Ralph Monthermer (d.1325). Around the same time Joan had paid homage to Edward I for her lands, she requested her father knight Ralph for his service, and then around January 1297 they married in secret. Perhaps Joan of Acre had hoped that by marrying a knight and not a squire she could soften the blow when she would have to tell her father. It didn't. Edward I was enraged and sent Ralph to be held at Bristol Castle.

Joan and Ralph must have surely been a love-match as Ralph would have known it would anger the mighty Edward I. Which it did, with Edward I seizing Joan's lands and imprisoning Ralph in Bristol Castle. The Bishop of Durham attempted mediation and Joan sent her three daughters by Gilbert de Clare to their grandfather to appeal for clemency.[9] However, it was the fact that Joan addressed her father herself in July 1297 that seemed to soften Edward I. Unusually, her speech to her father was recorded by local monks in the *Opus Chronicorum* and reads: 'It is not considered ignoble or disgraceful for a great and powerful earl to join himself in legal marriage with a poor and lesser woman, therefore, in the same manner it is not reprehensible or difficult a thing for a countess to promote a gallant youth'.[10] Edward had a reputation of being lenient where his daughters were concerned, and after seeing that Joan also happened to be pregnant with Ralph's child, he soon relented and restored most (not all) of her lands, as well as releasing Ralph from Bristol Castle. Ralph and Joan paid homage on 2 August 1297 to the king and Joan's brother, the Prince Edward, with Ralph becoming known as Earl of Gloucester and Hereford in right of his wife.[11] When Joan died in 1307 the titles reverted back to Ralph's stepson, the rightful heir, Gilbert de Clare. Ralph remained loyal to Edward I, especially during the various Scots wars, and he and Joan went on to have two sons and two daughters together.[12]

Mary Monthermer (1298–c.1371) would marry Duncan, the tenth Earl of Fife. Joan Monthermer (b.1299) would become a nun at Amesbury, Wiltshire.[13] Thomas Monthermer (1301–1340), son and heir, married, as her second husband, Margaret Teyes, nee Braose, sometimes known as Brewes (c.1303–1349), who was the sister of Mary Braose, second wife of Thomas of Brotherton, and stepmother to Alice of Norfolk. In fact, it was the older brother of Mary and Margaret Braose, also called Thomas, who married Beatrice Mortimer, the young widow of Edward Brotherton, brother of Alice of Norfolk.[14] The daughter of Thomas Monthermer and Margaret, also called Margaret, married – as we saw in the previous chapter – John Montagu, brother of the 2nd Earl of Salisbury and nephew of Edward Montagu and whose son, also John, would eventually become the 3rd Earl of Salisbury. The youngest son of Joan and Ralph, Edward (1304–1339/40) never married, but it is likely he was familiar with Edward Montagu, his cousin by marriage, as they were both with the king in Antwerp in September 1338.[15] Edward Monthermer was also active in military service to his cousin Edward III, fighting as a banneret in 1334–1339, including leading a small force of five men at arms and six archers in January 1337, joining the forces of Salisbury and Arundel marching north to Berwick.[16] Edward Monthermer also supported his uncle Edmund, Earl of Kent, in the conspiracy to free Edward II, for whom the Earl of Kent was summarily executed under the regency of Mortimer and Isabella, in 1330.

Joan of Acre died suddenly in April 1307 and was buried at Clare Priory, Suffolk, a house founded by Richard de Clare in 1248. Her death has been attributed to childbirth with what would have been her ninth pregnancy – there are no details in the records of any illness, ailment or need for medical recipes, although this is not wholly unusual in the medieval world. However, Joan left no will, or none known of to date, and as late as 20 March 1307, a mere month before she died, herself and Ralph are recorded as having the king's permission to 'search the writs and memoranda of the exchequer' for extra finances.[17] Not the action of one who appears to be nearing death, so childbirth/pregnancy is the most likely explanation.

In 1904 two bodies were discovered during excavations of the ruins of Clare Priory at the behest of the previous owner of the site, Sir George Barker: one was female, the other a very tall male. They were long thought to be Lionel of Antwerp (1338–1368), third son of Edward III, and his first wife, Elizabeth de Burgh (1332–1363), daughter of William de Burgh and Maud of Lancaster and herself a great-granddaughter of Joan of Acre. However, Elizabeth de Burgh is buried at Bruisyard Priory.[18] The two burials discovered at Clare Priory, and reinterred in 1904 at the exalted position of what would have been the high altar, are now thought to be Joan of Acre and her son, Edward Monthermer, as records show they were both buried there, next to each other. Edward more than likely inherited the Plantagenet 'tall' gene, the one that earned royalty nicknames such as Longshanks for Edward I and Long Lionel for Lionel of Antwerp.[19] Lionel had died in Italy in October 1368, just four months after marrying his second wife, Violante Visconti, a daughter of a lord in Milan, with his will stating his body be returned to England for burial at Clare Priory,[20] although it is now known Lionel's heart and bones, as requested, were bought back from Italy to England and his remains reinterred at Clare: 'Henry of Lancaster, returning from his pilgrimage to Jerusalem, visits the tomb of, *ib*, [Lionel] ; his heart, by his own request, carried to England, and buried in the Austin Friary at Clare.'[21] An antiquarian description of Lionel's burial at Clare notes his final resting place amid the choir as 'too simple' for such a prince and in March 2016 a geophysical study of the groundwork at Clare shows a small and shallow burial site to the south of the choir altar. Consideration is given that the small burial area could hold a small container of Lionel's bones and heart; these remains would require just small caskets, not a full-size coffin.[22]

In 1347 a chantry college for five chaplains had been founded by Maud of Lancaster, Countess of Ulster, who had married the grandson of Joan of Acre, William de Burgh, 3rd Earl of Ulster (September 1312–June 1333). Maud's sister Blanche had married Sir Thomas Wake, brother-in-law to Edmund of Woodstock, Alice's uncle, and another sister, Joan of Lancaster, married John Mowbray, 3rd Baron Mowbray. It was Joan and John Mowbray's son and daughter, John and Blanche, who were originally betrothed to Audrey and Edward Montagu, the eldest two children of Alice of Norfolk, but went on to marry the Montagu cousins, John and Elizabeth Segrave.

Joan of Acre's grandson, William de Burgh, was murdered in Ireland aged just twenty, leaving a year-old daughter, Elizabeth de Burgh *suo jure* Countess of Ulster (1332–1363). His widow, Maud of Lancaster, was remarried to Ralph Ufford, younger brother of Robert, Earl of Suffolk and uncle by marriage to Elizabeth and Joan Montagu, Alice's two younger daughters. Ralph died in 1346, and in 1347 Maud took the veil at Campsea Ashe, the burial place of the Uffords. In 1369 Robert, 1st Earl of Suffolk, was buried there. Alice's youngest child, Joan Montagu, Countess of Suffolk, was buried there in 1375, and her husband, William Ufford, 2nd Earl of Suffolk, followed in 1382. Maud took the veil at Campsea Ashe in October 1347, and when she founded the chantry college there, it was for her two husbands, William de Burgh and Ralph Ufford, their parents, herself, her two daughters (one by each marriage) and other members of family and friends.

In 1353 the Campsea Ashe chantry was endowed by a manor and lands called Roke Hall, which had been in the Bursyerd (Bruisyard) family since at least 1281.[23] Between 1332 and 1353 Roke Hall came to be in the hands of the Uffords as the king granted a licence to transfer ownership to the chantry college at Campsea Ashe of 'Rokehalle of Brusyerd which is held of the king in chief'.[24] A mere seven years later, in August 1354, the chaplains and the nuns of Campsea Ashe petitioned the Bishop of Norwich to move the chantry college from Campsea to the town of Bruisyard. The chaplains didn't live in the Campsea Ashe priory but nearby, and they stated their issues rather marvellously: 'it is way too distant from the priory and the priests on that account not without reason repute it too great a burden in winter or rainy season to go so great a distance to celebrate the divine offices especially as they have appointed in old age and habitation in a healthy place and there say service where there is no conversation of women rather than by the choir of the nuns where it happens at times that they mutually impede one another by the noise of voices'.[25]

In February 1364 Edward III granted his son, Lionel of Antwerp, licence to dissolve the chantry chapel. Lionel stated, 'inasmuch as the warden and chaplains are seculars and go about in secular habit not bound to the observance of any religion and as it were wholly neglect the divine obsequies required by the foundation of the chantry whereby the possessions and benefices thereof are destroyed in many ways, he desires that this chantry and its possession to be transferred to an abbess and their successors in the same place of Bruseyerd Rokhalle'.[26] Finally, in October 1366, Bruisyard Abbey, thus founded from Campsey Ashe, was home to the [nuns] Minoresses of St Clare, one of only four Franciscan orders in England. In 1364 Maud of Lancaster had papal permission to leave the Augustinian Campsea Ashe and entered Bruisyard Abbey, where she died in 1377. Her only issue with Ralph Ufford, their daughter, Maud Ufford, who would become the Countess of Oxford, was also buried there in 1413.[27]

These three ladies, picked at random but with links to the Norfolk Plantagenets, show that despite being considered chattels, property and portions of land deals, they were intelligent, tough, resilient and could more than hold their own. They were astute enough to make their positions work for them. Thankfully, more history books are being written about these marvellous medieval ladies and long may that continue.

Afterword

The aim of this book was to bring Alice of Norfolk to the knowledge of the wider history-loving public, hoping that knowledge of her existence goes some way to negate her premature death. It is not intended as a dry, academic tome but a story based on known facts and what can be accumulated from this. As the reader may have noticed, details of Alice are rather thin on the ground, but by fleshing out what is known, as well as exploring those around her, this hopefully gives Alice some presence.

I believe that in early 1342 the lady of Wark Castle, the wife of the castellan, was Alice of Norfolk. Edward Montagu, despite his faults, was a professional soldier who had survived major battles such as Crécy, with the capability of violence needed for the episode recorded at Wark in January 1342 and was highly likely to have been the castellan at that time. The evidence shows he was partaking in that episode of the Scots war and Wark Castle was right in the midst of the fighting. It was also a Montagu stronghold, as we know. As the Earl of Salisbury was a prisoner abroad, Edward Montagu would be the natural defender of Wark; the only other male Montagu brother was a bishop and the earl's son was a mere thirteen years old. Why would the young Alice, probably a mother at this point, be staying in such a volatile situation? Well, why not? It wasn't unusual – look at Eleanor of Aquitaine or Eleanor of Castile, for example. Go back a bit further and you'll find the formidable Nicholaa de la Haye defending Lincoln Castle. It is much more plausible that this lady was Alice and not Catherine, the actual Countess of Salisbury at the time and often the lady remarked on in the history books. The earl was captive abroad so why would the countess be in a war zone when her husband wasn't in the country? After all, she had been busy arranging her son's marriage to Alice of Norfolk's cousin, Joan of Kent, who has also been suggested as the lady at Wark. Joan, noted for her beauty, was thirteen or fourteen at the most and had been recently married to the earl's son, William, who is also mentioned at being at Wark in 1341/42, although wrongly noted as the earl's nephew and not his son. It is quite feasible William Junior was in his uncle Edward Montagu's household, but Joan had just been through the furore of her bigamous marriage and most likely did not live with William at this time. She wasn't the wife of the castellan as William Junior wasn't the castellan.

Although one has to allow a margin of error regarding the chroniclers of the day, a lot of the time they are the only records we have. For example, le Bel's 'the noble lady of Salisbury' could easily have been Alice, she was noble in her own right and had married into the powerful Salisbury Montagus. Alice was, perhaps, more of a player on the medieval stage than she is remembered for today – I don't believe she sat at Bungay Castle from 1340–1350 just popping out her babies – though I don't believe Edward III was sick with love for the lady at Wark either; lust is the more likely motive. Despite his solid union and remarkable closeness with his wife, Queen Philippa, he was also young – twenty-nine during the Wark incident – and virile; he was known to enjoy the company of women, enjoying a 'gay life in jousts and tourneys and entertaining ladies' (*Scalacronica*, p88), which is where the French propaganda of the supposed rape stems from. Depending on what source you read, Edward III either had no infidelities at all, was very discreet when he did, or had frequent extra-marital liaisons. I'd say he was discreet and probably very careful. There is no evidence of illegitimate children throughout their marriage, until the last years of Queen Philippa's life, when he takes the famous Alice Perrers as mistress in his household and they had three children together. See Sharon Bennett Connolly's *www.historytheinterestingbits.com* and *www.englishmonarchs.co.uk* as well the book, *The Queen and the Mistress: The Women of Edward III* by Gemma Hollman, for further reading.

All of Alice's close female relations have gone down in history as being extremely attractive, and even allowing for the sycophantic chronicle writings, Alice was most likely very attractive. She was also young, and spirited enough to be at Wark – if the noble lady there was indeed her – and therefore would have been a nice surprise for Edward III to come across during times of fighting. After all, it is considered that her father was no favourite of his. I believe there is a possibility that Thomas of Brotherton may have suffered some cognitive damage due to his traumatic birth, and was pleased to see the genealogist Brad Verity had also considered this when I read his papers. It would explain Thomas' lack of business acumen, but it must be remembered that he was a capable soldier and appeared to have been a fair landlord with loyal retainers. Also, the fact noted in the chronicles that Edward III hadn't seen the noble lady since her wedding also fits in with a time span of just a few years, when he was away in Ghent, as opposed to the thirteen years – or thereabouts – since his best friend's wedding. I do not necessarily believe the rape story of the Countess of Salisbury later that year, and after studying the excellent writings of this event by Gransden and Dr Mortimer, I firmly believe that it was wartime French propaganda attempting to tenuously link both the Wark incident and the supposed rape story. Perhaps Edward III simply fancied the pants off his cousin Alice!

Which leads me to consider that Edward Montagu and Alice actually had a good marriage, at least for the first few years, and it was most definitely fruitful. There are no recorded incidents of anything suggestive of what would happen in June 1351, although this has to be tempered with the fact that not a lot is recorded about Alice, even in the archives. There are recorded incidents of Edward Montagu, though none involving Alice. The recorded incident of Edward's attack on his wife is brutal. Yes, we have seen that he was prone to violence in his life, but this wasn't unusual in the nobility of the fourteenth century. After researching this for over two years, I believe the attack was sudden and unplanned. Michael Packe's 1983 biography of Edward III is the only one to examine the attack on Alice and comes to the same assessment, although some of his writing is too descriptive and some of his 'facts' need careful consideration.

As noted in this book, Edward and Alice were living in unprecedented times of disease, hardship and socio-economic collapse, lending itself to fear. A build-up of these relevant variables would have pushed a lot of people to their limits, but I think what tipped the scales against poor Alice on that fateful day was either the death of Edward, their son and heir, loss of a new baby son, or the birth of another daughter. No surviving child is recorded if that was the case. I could of course, be completely wrong, seeing as Edward and two retainers of his were involved, with weapons. Another reason that points to the attack being an unplanned, emotional reaction was the fact that Edward, or his accomplices, didn't kill Alice there and then; they didn't finish the job so to speak, if it was planned. She'd be able to identify them for a start. And although the Ancient Indictment detailing Alice's attack was held in Suffolk, it does seem as though Edward was likely in London on 19 January 1352, right at the time she was dying/died. I believe that she had died by then and he was in London to answer to his actions. With the exception of being summoned to his nephew's retinue in 1355/6, under the orders of the Black Prince in the lead up to the Battle of Poitiers in 1356, Edward appears not to have gone abroad on business for the king again until his death in 1361. There seem to be no charges against him for Alice's death either, but as Dr Ian Mortimer notes, Alice was his property at the end of the day, in the eyes of the law, despite being the king's cousin, and they had common offspring. As one of his retainers, William Dunch, was pardoned for the attack on Alice shortly before Edward died, it is likely he took most of the punishment. The other accomplice, Thomas the priest, should have been questioned by the church, but I have found no evidence so far.

The problem is that trying to analyse the little information available tends to raise more questions. Here's hoping that more evidence comes to light in the not-too-distant future and that some more flesh can appear on the bones of Alice Plantagenet of Norfolk and make her a complete person again. It would be nice to write about her without all the ifs and buts.

Appendix I

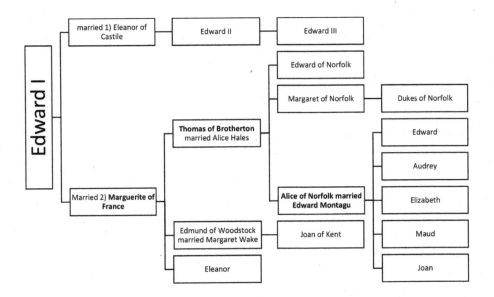

Appendix II

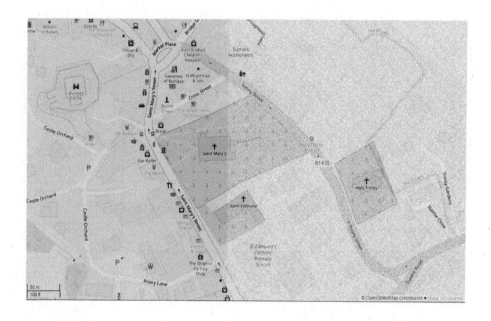

Notes

Introduction

1. Marshall (2006b), p5
2. Ben Johnson, Historic UK (online)
3. Sharp Buchanan, Royal paternalism and the moral economy in the reign of Edward II: the response to the Great Famine, p629
4. *Ibid;* Campbell, p293
5. William Chester Jordan, The Great Famine 1315–1322 Revisited, p51
6. Horrox, Ormrod, p119
7. Jessop, p201
8. *Ibid* p186
9. Pobst v1, p.xxxi
10. Dittmar *et al* p21
11. Podd, pp128–9
12. Ridgard, pp4–5
13. Jonker p106; Mawhinney p64
14. Edward III Year Books, v11, p5; CPR 1343-1345, p450

Chapter 1: The Murdered Granddaughter Alice of Norfolk

1. Danièle Cybulskie, Childhood in the Middle Ages [online]
2. Leyser, p133; Ward, pp19–20
3. Swabey, p33; Jonker, pp105–117
4. Mortimer (2009), p37
5. Wilson-Lee, pp31–33; Forser & Yuveri; Phillips p52
6. ODNB
7. Hollman, pp64–65
8. ODNB
9. Wilson-Lee, Family Tree; Bennett-Connolly, p10
10. Ward, p40, pp113–7; Leyser, p107.
11. CPR 1330-1334, p402
12. CIPM 1336-1346, pp154–55; CPMR 1337-1344 pp165–197
13. Parker, p71
14. *Ibid* p38
15. TNA SC 8/278/13885
16. ODNB
17. Warner K (2019) *The Life and Tragic Death of Alice of Norfolk* (online); Verity, p99
18. Parker p38
19. Wrottesley (1898), 196
20. Parker, 1985; Packe, pp175–178
21. CPR 1334-1338, p401

22. CPR 1338-1340, p192
23. CPR 1321-1324, p187
24. Wrottesley pp84–95, p196; Hefferan pp24–29; Gascony Rolls C61/67 (1355–1356). See membrane 7 for letters of protection and membrane 10 for appointing attorneys
25. CP v9, p84
26. CFR 1337-1347 p111; CIPM 1361-1365, no.545
27. CClR 1349-1354, p112
28. ODNB
29. TNA BCM/D/1/1/9,11
30. Halliwell, p310
31. CIPM 1352-1361, no.564; Calendar of Papal Registers 1342–1362, pp319–338; Warner K (2019) op.cit
32. Jessop, p213
33. Mann, p84
34. Pobst, p96, no.590
35. *Ibid* pp97–98, no.605
36. Mann, pp84–85
37. CIPM 1361-1365, no.140
38. CP v7, p302
39. CPR 1350-1354, p108
40. TNA BCM/D/3
41. TNA SC 8/269/13446; CClr 1360-1364, p148
42. CClR p 329; CP v2 p7; Richardson p637; Nichols, p 273; Weir, p88
43. Page & Horace, pp115–122
44. CPR 1361-1364, p234
45. CPR 1374-1377, p449; CPR 1391-1396, p317; CIPM 1361-1365 no.516
46. CP v7, p302
47. ODNB
48. Waters pp328–330
49. Parker, p19
50. CPR 1281-1292, p.1
51. Judith Green p378
52. ODNB; CIPM 1316-1327, p44; CClR 1318-1318 p542; Parker, p20
53. CPR 1321-1324 p187
54. Parker p7
55. Marshall (2006b), p142
56. CPR 1330-1334, p74
57. CClR 1360-1364, p455; CPR 1370-1374 p150; CP v7 p303
58. FF CP 25/1/142/137, no.24
59. CP v7, p302; Nichols v2, p273
60. Chronica Maiora, p173
61. Gilchrist & Olivia p40; p90
62. CIPM 1291-1300, p389; ODNB; Parker, p240; Page (1975a), pp112–115
63. CClR 1349-1354 p140; CPR 1348-1350, p447
64. Bailey (2009) pp25–31; CPR 1350-1354, p24
65. Bolton, p218
66. McAndrew, p119, p132
67. Day, pp146–148
68. Bailey (2019)

69. CFR 1347-1356, p288
70. CPR 1350-1354, p181
71. CPR 1350-1354, p184
72. Dugdale (1685), p264
73. CClR 1349-1354, p459
74. CFR 1347-1356, p345
75. CClR 1349 - 1354, p411–412; CPR 1350 - 1354, p230
76. TNA KB9
77. Butler (2007) p35
78. Mount p66; Butler (2007) p71; Hawkes, Chapter 2
79. Butler (2001) pp61–78
80. CClR 1349-1354, p361
81. Pobst no.206, no.1573
82. Pobst, Bishop of Norwich Registers v1 and v2
83. CClR 1339-1341, p39 – 40; Pobst no.1710-11
84. Northeast, p5; Geocache.co.uk; White, p441
85. CPR 1361-1364, p26
86. CPR 1361-1364, p38; Wrottesley, p36; Hefferan p46
87. Musson & Powell, pp70–73; see all of Chapter 3 for examples from the records.
88. CPR 1345-1348, p125
89. CPR 1345-1348, p153
90. Thompson, p143; Aberth pp283–301
91. CPR 1348-1350, p. 464
92. CPR 1358-61, p563
93. Thompson, p145
94. Briggs, p120. For more social statistics of the plague, see chapter 4
95. Kitzinger, 2012
96. CPR 1350-1354, p285
97. Foedera III, i, pp284–285
98. *Ibid*, p337
99. CIPM 1361-1365 n.140
100. Simon Knott *Suffolk Churches*
101. Suffolk Heritage Explorer *Record Number BUN 006*
102. CChR 1327-1341 pp225–226
103. CChR 1226-1257 p195
104. Mortimer (1981) pp1–16; CP v9, p586; Bailey 1948 pp84–103
105. Mann p36; pp101–102; White, p428
106. Suckling pp119–161; Mann p36
107. Mann, p45
108. Suckling, p149; TNA C143/381/8; CPR1370-1374 p361
109. Mann, p5
110. *Index Monasticus*, p87
111. Mann p40, p75; Suckling
112. Bennett Connolly (2017), pp11–12
113. Mount, pp68–70

Chapter 2: The Powerful Granddaughter Margaret

1. CIPM 1362-1365, p306
2. CPR 1327-1330, p23

3. Warner K (2012b) *19 October 1330: Edward III's Arrest Of Roger Mortimer* (online)
4. ODNB
5. *Ibid*
6. *Ibid*
7. Warner, K (2010a) *The Children Of Richard Fitzalan, Earl Of Arundel* (online); CClR 1323-1327 p13
8. Carter, pp1623–1626; Wyatt, p17
9. ODNB; CIPM 1316-1327 no.700; TNA BCM/D/7
10. TNA BCM/D.5.1/17
11. CIM 1348-1377 (v3), no.50
12. Sumption, p17; KW 2016
13. ODNB; Marshall (2006b)
14. CP v7 p103; CIPM 1352-1361, no.116
15. Archer, pp266–267; CClR 1354-1360, p27; CPR 1354 - 1358, p325
16. Bateson pp56–57
17. Sandford (1677) p.208; Weever (1767) p216; Beltz (1841) p122
18. Wilson-Lee, p336
19. CIPM 1352-1361, no121; TNA BCM/D/5/101/8
20. Ward (1992), p13
21. CPR 1367-1370, p237
22. Richardson, 2002 (Richardson notes the cited charter is available at *Miscellanea Genealogica et Heraldica*, 5th series, no.9 (1935–37): 48); Richardson, (2011) *Plantagenet Ancestry*, p.xix
23. CPR 1367-1370, p236
24. CIPM 1365-1370, no.397
25. CP v9, p780
26. CIPM 1399-1405 no.268
27. Stevenson (1836), p.iv
28. CFR 1405-1414, p161
29. CCR 1435-1441, p76; Verity, *Chronology of Brotherton/Segrave/Mowbray*, Roskell *et al* (1993)
30. CIPM 1365-1370 no.397; Coucher Book of Furness Abbey, p292
31. ODNB; RotP Vol 3, p383
32. Archer, p278; ODNB
33. Bennett Connolly *Blanche* [online]; Verity *Chronology*
34. TNA BCM/D/5/101/8 & BCM/D/1/1/13-14; Verity *Chronology*
35. CIPM 1370-1373, no.148
36. *Calender of Papal Registers* 1362–1404, pp66–71
37. Weir, p115
38. Warner, K (2022) *Margaret of Norfolk* (online); ODNB
39. CIPM 1384-1392, no.11
40. ODNB; CPR 1388-92, p469
41. McKisack, p261; Archer, p267
42. Archer, p268; *Ancient Petitions of Wales*, p448; ODNB
43. CPR 1377-1399, p408; CIM 1387-1393, p136
44. CIM 1387-1393, p137; TNA C/47/10/33/11
45. Rigard p86; Wyatt (2018) p58
46. GGAT (Magor); Wyatt (2019a); Nayling
47. *Testamenta Vetusta* p80

48. *Ibid*, p132
49. Archer p274; English Heritage; Mitchell, pp137–138
50. ODNB
51. Kingsford, p7, pp15–16
52. *Ibid*, p7, p40
53. *Testamenta Vetusta*, p55; CIPM 1316-1327, no.700; Serjeantson & Adkins, pp133–135
54. *Testamenta Vetusta* p85
55. Platt, p180; Cockburn *et al* pp159–169
56. CPR 1370-1374, p44
57. ODNB; Cockburn *et al* pp159–169

Chapter 3: Thomas of Brotherton, Earl of Norfolk
1. Weir, p82; Morris, pp3–4
2. Morris, p20
3. Phillips, pp89–90
4. Hilton, p201; English Heritage; Dr E Hallam, p18
5. Morris, pp230–231
6. Langtoft v2, pp316–317
7. Wilson-Lee, p200; CPR 1301-1307, p38
8. Marshall (2006a), p202
9. Bennet-Connolly, *History, the Interesting Bits.*
10. ODNB
11. Wilson-Lee, p200
12. Verity, p92; Staniland, pp6–7
13. Hilton, p206
14. Staniland, p7; Prestwich (1997), p131
15. Rishanger, p438
16. Langtoft v2, p325
17. Mee, p87
18. ODNB; Rishanger pp438–9
19. Staniland, p13
20. Warner, K (2010b) *Marguerite Of France (1)* (online); CPR 1301-1307, p431; ODNB
21. Verity, p93; Marshall pp192–194; CClR 1296-1302 p416; TNA E101/360/15
22. Morris, pp361–2
23. Weir, pp82–90
24. CChRolls 1300-1326, p205
25. CPR 1307-1313, p272; Foedera, v2, p111
26. Foedera, v2, p102
27. Warner, K (2020), *Jousting 1323* (online)
28. Verity, p93; CPR 1301-1307, p460
29. Warner, K (2015) *Marriage Negotiations between England and Aragon in Edward II's Reign* (online); AM p78
30. Baigent, p410
31. Feet of Fines (Norfolk), no.936, p161; Verity *Chronology.*
32. Marshall (2006b), p78; Marshall (2008) p1; Benz, pp105–6
33. CPR 1301-1307, p170
34. CPR 1327-1330, p508
35. CPR 1345-1348, p125, 153; Wrottesley (1898), p82

36. Pobst v1, n.206, p50
37. Verity (2006) p98; Marshall (2006b), pp138–9; Warner (2015) op.cit
38. Verity (2006) p99
39. Mortimer (2006), p225, p323
40. CPR 1334-1338, p62
41. Verity (2006) p98; Betham, p130; Warner, K (2013b) *Thomas of Brotherton's wedding, his daughter Margaret and his grandchildren* (online); Marshall (2006b), p147
42. CPR 1324-1327, p267
43. CPR 1330-1334, p11
44. Verity *Chronology* quoting Suffolk Record Office HD 1538/202/1/128 and *Miscellanea Genealogica et Heraldica* series 5, v9, p166; CP v2, pp308–309
45. CClR 1337-1339 p256
46. CFR 1319-1327, p68
47. ODNB; Warner, K (2014b) *The Children of Edmund of Woodstock and Margaret Wake, and Joan of Kent's Date of Birth* (online)
48. *Froissart*, Book 1, f2v
49. CPR 1327-1330, p268
50. ODNB
51. CClR 1330-1333, p400
52. CPR 1334-1338, p426, p434; Thompson, p72; Marshall (2008), p3
53. CClR 1337-39 p79; CFR 1337 - 1347 pp91–2; Marshall (2006b) pp125–6; Jones W.R pp1–29
54. CClR 1337-1339 p232, 281
55. CPR 1338–1340, p7, 55, 57, 61, 93, 97, 104–5
56. Verity (2006), p109; CP v9, p598; CIPM 1336-1347, no.195
57. Childs, pp198–9
58. Nalivaeva *et al* (2018)
59. Marshall (2006a), p203
60. CPR 1327-1330, pp213–4
61. The Suffolk Institute of Archeaology and History Proceedings (1859) pp90–94
62. Weever (1767), p465.
63. Martin *et al* (2001) p210

Chapter 4: Edward II and the Norfolk Plantagenets

1. Given-Wilson, p97; Marshall (2006b) Thomas' lack of presence is noted in the Abstract
2. ODNB; Given-Wilson, p5
3. Wilson-Lee, pp254–256
4. *Ibid* p297
5. *Ibid* pp255–257
6. CCR 1302-1307, p342
7. Childs, *Vita*, pxxxv; Wilson-Lee, pp254 -256
8. ODNB; Given-Wilson, p10
9. Kathryn Warner (2006) see *The Feast of the Swan, 22 May 1306* (online)
10. Given-Wilson, p11; ODNB
11. Higden p299; *Vita* p5
12. Warner,K (2008b) *Edward II's Chamber Journal, 1322–1323* (online); Given-Wilson, p4
13. Wilson-Lee, p285; Prestwich (2005), p178

14. *Vita* pp7–9
15. Marshall (2006b), p48
16. Hilton, pp211–212
17. Warner,K (2014a) *Edward II, Piers Gaveston and Isabella's Jewels That Weren't* (online); McKisack, p4
18. CFR 1307 – 1319, p14
19. Given-Wilson, p15; Anerje (2012)
20. *Vita* p29
21. Verity, p93; Marshall (2006b), p170
22. CPR 1301-1307, p460
23. CChR 1300-1326, p205–6; CClR 1307-1313, p295
24. CCR 1307-1313, pp448–9; ODNB
25. *Vita* p21
26. McKisack, p10, n2
27. ODNB; McKisack, pp10–12; Warner, K (2012a) *Stay Away From The King, You Gascons (The Ordinaces)* (online)
28. Hilton, p213
29. Prestwich (1997), p130
30. CPR 1317-1321, p38, p46
31. ODNB; Warner (2010c) *Marguerite of France (2)* (online); *Foedera* ii, p360
32. Marshall (2006b), p47; CPR1301-1307, p47; *Vita* p199
33. Prestwich (2005), p201
34. *Vita*, p199; Marshall (2006b), p76; McKisack, p66
35. Wilson-Lee, pp218–219
36. *Ibid,* p301
37. CClR 1318-1323, pp505–6
38. McKisack, pp74–75; Marshall (2006b), pp79–81
39. Marshall (2006b), p78
40. Given-Wilson, pp89–90
41. *Vita,* p235
42. ODNB; Given-Wilson, pp92–3
43. Notes & Queries, p258; CPR 1324-1337, p267
44. McKisack, p83; ODNB
45. *Brut*, p237
46. Warner, K (2017a) *Edward II. The Unconventional King. See all of chapter 15.*
47. Given-Wilson, p94; ODNB; Sumption, p18
48. Margary, p40
49. The Berkeley Manuscripts, pp286–287
50. CClR 1326-1327 pp655–6; Le Bel, pp21–24
51. Warner (2017a), *Edward II. The Unconventional King*. See all of chapter 15; Brut, p240
52. Given-Wilson, pp95–96; Hilton, p238; Harding, p16

Chapter 5: Edward III and the Norfolk Plantagenets

1. Wyatt (2018), p19
2. Warner, K (2007a) *Birthday Wishes, Mortimer Ancestry, and Joan de Geneville* (online); ODNB; English Heritage
3. Dryburgh, p75
4. McKisack, p62

5. CClR 1318-1323, pp493–4
6. CPR 1321-1324, p15, p17
7. CClR 1318-1323, pp505–6; Dryburgh, pp79–80
8. McKisack, pp96–97; Mortimer (2008) see chapter 14; Hilton, p243
9. ODNB
10. Marshall (2006b) p114; (2006a) pp190, 193, 199–200; Orme, p178
11. Murimuth, pp59–60; Warner (2011b) pp803–804, *The Adherents of Edmund Woodstock*
12. Mortimer (2010), p163
13. Warner (2011b), op.cit, p800; Marshall (2006b), p12
14. CPR 1327-1330, p508
15. CCR, 1330-1333, p141, p153; Bothwell (2004) p64
16. Marshall (2006b), p122
17. Hilton p244; Mortimer (2008) *see chapter 14*; McKisack, pp100–101
18. Foedera II, ii, 787
19. PRME
20. Parker, pp32–33; PRME; Warner, K (2012b) *19 October 1330: Edward III's Arrest Of Roger Mortimer* (online)
21. CClR 1330-1333, p153; PRME
22. Marshall (2006b), p121
23. Mortimer, ch14; PRME
24. Mortimer (2014) *A note on the deaths of Edward II*; KW (2013a) *Edward II's Death And Afterlife Revisited (2)*1; Mortimer (2010), pp56–58
25. Warner (2007b) *The Conspiracy of the Earl of Kent, 1330 (3)* (online); *Murimuth* pp255–257
26. Bothwell (2004) p5; Thompson p72
27. Marshall (2006b), p204; ODNB
28. Bothwell (2004), pp15–16
29. Bothwell (2004) pp23–24; Parker, 1985, pp19–20
30. ODNB; Bothwell (2004) pp24–25; CP v9 pp81–82
31. Parker, pp15–17; ODNB
32. CPR 1330-1334, p179
33. ODNB
34. Le Bel, p78
35. Marshall (2006b), p204
36. Richard Carlton, No.24: *Archaeological Fieldwork at Wark-on-Tweed, 2013 and 2015*; see *Scotland*, chapter 9 in *Plantagenet England* by Michael Prestwich (2005) for more info on Wark Castle and its strategical use.
37. Mortimer 2008 chapter 8, ref: 38 quoting TNA E36/204/f.20v
38. Prestwich (2005), p311
39. Le Bel, p123
40. *Ibid*, p125
41. *Ibid*, p127
42. *Ibid*, p146; Packe, p118
43. *Ibid*, p146
44. *Ibid*, pp155–156; Mortimer (2008) see chapter 8 – *Chivalry and Shame* for a complete critiqued analysis of this story.
45. Mortimer *Ibid*; Packe, pp116–117; CPR 1327-1330, p392; CPR 1330-1334, p462; CPR 1334-1338, p162

46. Foedera II, ii, p1225
47. Beltz p.xlv; Lettenhove, p516
48. Dugdale (1675), *Baronage of England*, p653
49. Foedera II, ii, p1181
50. Betham, p130
51. Bennett-Connolly, *The Fascinating Marital Exploits of Joan, the Fair Maid of Kent* (online)
52. Mortimer (2008) Op. cit; Packe, p115; CP v9, p84
53. Mortimer (2008) Op. cit, p43
54. Gransden, pp340–341
55. Murimuth, p128; Mortimer (2008), see chapter 8, p45
56. Gransden; Mortimer *Ibid.*
57. Le Bel (Bryant), p1
58. Tyson, 1986
59. ODNB
60. Gransden, p344

Chapter 6: The Montagu Family

1. Burrow, p139; ODNB
2. CP v9, p75; *Drogo of Montactue* see https://opendomesday.org
3. CP *Ibid;* Page (1906), pp383–432
4. Barlow p109; Stubbs, p4
5. Prior pp87–89
6. Freeman (1873), pp272–3, p278; Montacute Cartulary, p125, no.9; Page (1911) pp111–115
7. ODNB; CP v9 p75
8. CClR 1279-1288, p9
9. Musson, p6
10. ODNB; CP v9, p78
11. Stapleton, p. 339
12. *Testamenta Vestusta* pp124–5; CP v9, p88
13. Bennett-Connolly *William Montagu, the Man Who Married – and Lost – the Fair Maid of Kent* (online); Mark Warner (1991), p81
14. Wrottesley (1898), p35, p55
15. ODNB; Richardson *Magna Carta Ancestry*, p272
16. *Register of Simon de Montacute*, pxvii; *Feodera* II, p379
17. CClR 1343-1346, p451, p456; CClR 1368-1374, p518; *Norton Bavant*, pp47–58
18. CPR 1348-1350, p65, p173, pp237–238
19. CPR 1334-1338 pp92–93
20. CClR 1354-1360 p99, p213
21. CPR 1354-1358, p383; Bird (1922), pp153–187
22. *Register of Simon de Montacute*, pxviii; ODNB
23. FoF CP25/1/138/101 no.34; CPR 1345-1348, p146
24. Page & Horace (1907) pp115–122
25. Warner, K (2011a) *William Montacute, Another Royal Favourite (1)* (online); Wright (1836), p225; CP v4, p97; *Stemmata Robertson et Durdin* pp96–97; St Frideswide Cartulary, p9, p15
26. Alamo & Pendergast, pp82–87; Bloxham pp150–157
27. CClR 1333-1337, p105

28. CPR 1334-1338, p401
29. Verity (2006) family tree; Mark Warner (1991) p37
30. CIPM 1336-1347, No.195
31. CFR 1319-1327, p133
32. Wyatt (2019), p21; elydiocese.org
33. CIPM 1361-1365, No.140 & 141; Richardson *Plantagenet*, p637; Weir p87
34. Dugdale (1685), p262, p264
35. Wrottesley (1905), p113, p133
36. CIPM 1384 – 1392, no.1029, 1030
37. Kerry, p108, p117
38. CP v9, pp85–6; Richardson (2007), *Narkive*; TNA SC 8/176/8788
39. CPR 1374-1377, p490; History of Suffolk Volume 1, pp119 - 161; Eileen Power, n.1378, pp436–446
40. CP v9; *Testament Vestusta* p124
41. CPR 1405-1409 pp455–456; CP v9, p83

Chapter 7: Plantagenent Women
Joan of Kent

1. Lawne (2006), p5
2. Warner (2014b) *The Children of Edmund of Woodstock and Margaret Wake, and Joan of Kent's Date of Birth* (online)
3. CFR 1327-1337, p277
4. CIPM 1352-1361, see p42 for birthdate of 1326 and p45 for 1327
5. CIPM 1347-1352, no.673, p455
6. Gascon Rolls C61/52 m23, No.12
7. *Feodera* II, ii, p1119
8. Delmas-Marsalet (2016) *Albret*, no.44; Warner (2014b) op. cit; Lawne (2006), p113
9. Podd, pp123–4
10. CIPM 1347-1352, no.219, 234
11. CFR 1327-1337, p277
12. Warner (2017b) *Thomas, Lord Wake (1298–1349)* [online]
13. CFR 1327-1337, p175
14. CPR 1327-1330, p499
15. Lawne (2006), p51; CClR 1330-1333, p14
16. CPR 1330-1334, p20
17. Bennett-Connolly, *The Fascinating Marital Exploits of Joan, the Fair Maid of Kent* [online]
18. CPR 1330-1334, p99, p109, p193
19. Wentersdorf, pp203–231; Wrottesley (1898), p33
20. Lawne (2006) p74; Lawne (2016) *see Chapter 5 for a detailed description*
21. Mark Warner (1991), p40; ODNB
22. CPR 1340-1343, p145
23. Wentersdorf, p215
24. CPR 1345-1348, p431
25. *Calendar of Papal Registers* 1342–1362, p252
26. Wentersdorf, pp203–231; Lawne (2006) pp106–109
27. Lawne (2006) p109; CP v9 24; Holmes, p27
28. Wentersdorf, p219; *Foedera* III, ii, p626
29. Chandos Herald, p.vi; p106
30. Bennett-Connolly op.cit; Weir pp93–94; ODNB; Wentersdorf, p219

Mary of Woodstock, Nun-Princess
1. Green, p406; Bennett-Connolly *Mary of Woodstock, Royal Nun* [online]
2. Feodera I, p651
3. Wilson-Lee, pp57–66
4. Platt, p1
5. Weir pp20–21; Pugh & Crittal, pp242–259
6. CClR 1279-1288, p14
7. *Ibid*, p96
8. Platt, p3; Wilson-Lee, p59
9. Hilton, p188
10. McAleavy, 1996
11. Barefield pp21–30; Bennett-Connolly op.cit; Hilton, pp197–8
12. CPR 1301-1307, p19, p52
13. Marshall (2006a), p202
14. See *gatehouse.gazeetter.info* for more Ludgershall Castle
15. Wilson-Lee, p209, p236; Panton, p322
16. Wilson-Lee, pp275–278
17. Barefield, pp21–30
18. Green, p441; CClR 1330 – 1333, p511; Wilson-Lee, p300
19. Green, p442

Joan of Acre (1272–1307)
1. ODNB; Warner (2008a) *Sisters of Edward II (2): Joan of Acre* (online)
2. CPR 1292-1301, p592, p606
3. *Vita* p93; Prestwich (2005) p257
4. Warner, K (2008a) op.cit; Weir, p84
5. Wilson-Lee, p149
6. CClR 1288-1296, pp470–71; Fleming, p11
7. Wilson-Lee, pp149–60
8. Bennett Connolly (2017), pp213–214; Prestwich (2005) p364
9. Bennett Connolly (2017), p215
10. Wilson-Lee, p178
11. CFR 1272-1307, p389
12. ODNB
13. Warner (2008a), op.cit.
14. Verity (2006), pp105–107
15. ODNB; CPR 1338-1340, p192
16. Parker, p92, p123
17. CClR 1302-1307, pp495–496
18. TNA E101/394/19/001
19. Ashdown-Hill *The problems of Richard III's Y chromosome* [online]; Jarvis, H Rev (1886–1887), p80
20. *Testament Vestusta*, p70
21. *Liber de illustribus Henricis*, p100, p299
22. Weever, pp472–479; Ashdown-Hill, op.cit.
23. Suckling, pp101–103; Pobst (1996) v1, No.3
24. CPR 1350-1354, p399;
25. CPR 1354-1358, pp484–486; Allen, pp151–174
26. CPR 1361-1364, p463
27. ODNB; Allen, op.cit.

Bibliography

Primary Sources
Calendar of Close Rolls (CClR)
Calendar of Charter Rolls (CChR)
Calendar of Fine Rolls (CFR)
Calendar of Inquisitions Miscellaneous (CIM)
Calendar of Inquisitions Post Mortem (CIPM)
Calendar of Papal Registers
Calendar of Patent Rolls (CPR)
Complete Peerage (CP)
Gwent-Glamorgan Archaeological Trust (GGAT)
Oxford Dictionary of National Biography (ODNB)
The National Archives (TNA)

Adae Murimuth Continuatio Chronicarum edited by Edward Maunde Thompson. Rolls
   Series (1889)
Berkeley Manuscripts in *The Lords of the Honour, Castle and Manor of Berkeley from 1066–
   1618*. Volume 1 by John Smyth of Nibley (1628). Ed. Sir John Maclean (1883). Bristol
   and Gloucestershire Archaeological Society: John Bellows
Brut Chronicle, I and II ed. Brie (1906). Available at archive.org
Cambridge Gild Records. Bateson, M (1903) ed. Available at archive.org.
Chronica et Annales by William Rishanger
Chronica Maiora of Thomas Walsingham 1376–1422 – ed by Preest and Clark (2005),
   Boydell Press
Chronicle of Pierre de Langtoft, Volume 2. Edited by Thomas Wright (1868). Available at
   https://.babelhathitrust.org)
Coucher Book of Furness Abbey Volume 2 (1916) available at https://babel.hathitrust.org/
Dugdale, W (1675) *The Baronage of England*. Available at Early English Books Online
Dugdale, W (1685) *A Perfect Copy of All Summons of the Nobility to the Great Councils and
   Parliaments of this Realm*. Available at archive.org
Feet of Fines CP 25/1/138/101, number 34; CP25/1/142/137 no.24. Available at www.
   medievalgenealogy.org.uk/
Halliwell J (1889) *A Dictionary of Archaic and Provincial Words, Obsolete Phrases, Proverbs,
   and Ancient Customs, from the Fourteenth Century v1*. LONDON: Reeves and Turner
Index Monasticus. Taylor, R.C (1821) London
Kingsford, C.L (1915) *The Greyfriars of London, their history with the Register of their
   Convent and an appendix of documents*. Aberdeen: The University Press
Lanercrost Chronicle 1272–1346 – tr. Sir Herbert Maxwell GLASGOW: Glasgow uni
   Press. 1913

Liber de illustribus Henricis by John Capgrave (1393-1464) ed. F.C Hingeston (1858)

Montacute Cartulary. Available at archive.org

Nicholas Trevet Annales Sex Regum Angliae ed. Thomas Hogg (1845) Available at archive. org

Notes & Queries (1849) Seventh Series, Volume 2. Available at archive.org

Polychronicon by Ranulph Higden (c.1342). Available at www.archive.org

Register of Simon de Montacute Bishop of Worcester 1334–1337 by Roy Martin Haines of Clare Hall, Cambridge. The Worcestershire Historical Society.

Robertson, H (1893) *Stemmata Robertson et Durdin*. London: Mitchell & Hughes

Rotuli Parliamentorum available on Google Books

Sandford, F (1677) *A genealogical history of the kings of England, and monarchs of Great Britain, from the Conquest 1066, to the year 1677*. London: Savoy. Available at archive.org

Scalacronica by Sir Thomas Grey. Ed. By J Stevenson (1836) Glasgow: Maitland Club

St Frideswide Cartulary Vol 2, ed. Spencer R. Wigram (1895). Oxford: Clarendon Press

Testamenta Vestusta. Available at https://babel.hathitrust.org

The Topographer and Genealogist volume 2. J Nichols (1853)

The Battle Rolls. Volume 2 pp284–286. Available at archive.org

The True Chronicles of Jean le Bel 1290–1360. Translated by Nigel Bryant (2011) Woodbridge: Boydell Press

Vita Edwardi Secundii – ed.Wendy Childs (2005) OXFORD: Clarendon Press.

Wright, T (1836) *The History and Topography of the County of Essex Volume 1*. London: George Virtue

Year books of the reign of King Edward the Third v11 1883 (available on archive.org)

Online Resources

www.historyofparliament.org.uk

www.archive.org

www.fmg.ac

www.edwardthesecond.blogspot

www.historytheinterestingbits.com

https://opendomesday.org/

http://www.gatehouse-gazetteer.info/

www.haithitrust.org

www.charterhouse.org.uk (History & Archives)

www.english-heritage.org.uk

www.geocache.co.uk (Dunche's Lane)

www.cracroftspeerage.co.uk

www.britainexpress.com

https://Stmaryschurchbungay.co.uk

Unpublished Sources

Barking Abbey [dissertation]. Available at www.repository.cam.ac.uk

Benz, L (2009) *Queen Consort, Queen Mother: The Power and Authority of Fourteenth-Century Plantagenet Queens*. University of York: Department of History [thesis]

Delmas-Marsalet, C (2016) *Albret Geneaology* (Centre Généalogique des Landes).

Dryburgh, P (2002) *The career of Roger Mortimer, first earl of March (c.1287-1330)*. University of Bristol [thesis]

Harding, David Anthony (1985) *The regime of Isabella and Mortimer 1326–1330*. Durham University. [thesis] Available at: http://etheses.dur.ac.uk/7483/

Lawne, P (2006) *Joan of Kent, daughter of Edmund of Woodstock: Royal Kinship and Marriage in the Fourteenth Century* (Royal Holloway College). University of London. [thesis]

Marshall, A (2006b). *Thomas of Brotherton, Earl of Norfolk and Marshal of England : a study in early fourteenth-century aristocracy*. University of Bristol. [thesis]

Mawhinney, S Dr (2015) *Coming of Age: Youth in England, c.1400-1600* University of York [thesis].

McAndrew, D. (2008) *The catalysts and constraints of castle-building in Suffolk c.1066-1200*. University of London. [thesis]. Available at https://discovery.ucl.ac.uk

Parker, Jennifer Mary (1985) *Patronage and service: the careers of William Montagu, earl of Salisbury, William Clinton, earl of Huntingdon, Robert Ufford, earl of Suffolk and William Dohun, earl of Northampton*. Durham University. [thesis] Available at http://etheses.dur.ac.uk/7041/

Phillips, K.M (1997) *The Medieval Maiden: Young Womanhood in Late Medieval England*. University of York Centre for Medieval Studies. [thesis]

Prior, S (2004) *'Winning Strategies' An Archaeological Study of Norman Castles in the Landscapes of Somerset, Monmouthshire & Co. Meath, 1066-1186*. Vol 1 & 2. University of Bristol [thesis]

Thompson, M (2014) *All The King's Men: Chivalry and Knighthood in England 1327-77*. The University of Hull: [PhD thesis]

Verity, B *Chronology of Brotherton/Segrave/Mowbray* (unpublished)

Warner, Mark (1991) *The Montagu Earls of Salisbury circa 1300–1428*. University College London. [PHd Thesis]

Day, Rosemary (2020) *Architectural and economic development on three groups of estates in Suffolk, Norfolk and Essex between 1066 and the early fourteenth century*. Birkbeck: University of London. [thesis]

Secondary Sources

Aberth, J (1992) Crime and Justice under Edward III: The Case of Thomas De Lisle. *The English Historical Review*. Volume 107(423) pp283-301. Oxford University Press

Alamo E; Pendergast C (2020) ed. *Memory and the Medieval Tomb*. Oxon: Routledge

Allen, D (2014) A newly discovered survival from the muniments of Maud of Lancaster's Chantry College at Bruisyard. In *Suffolk Institute of Archaeology and History* Volume XLI(2), pp151-174

Altschul, M (1965) *A Baronial Family in Medieval England: The Clares, 1217-1314*. USA: John Hopkins University Press (2019)

Anerje (2012) *The Coronation of Edward II*. Available at https://piersperrotgaveston.blogspot.com/

Archer, R (1987) The Estates and Finances of Margaret of Brotherton, c.1320–1399. *Historical Research* Volume 60(143), pp 264-280

Ashdown-Hill, J (2017) *The problems of Richard III's Y chromosome; the problems relating to the burials at Clare Priory, and the problems of working with Historic England*. Available at https://nerdalicious.com.au/ [article]

Baigent, F. J (1897). *The Registers of John de Sandale and Rigaud de Asserio, bishops of Winchester 1316–1323*. London: Simpkin

Bailey, M. (2019) *Society, economy and the law in fourteenth-century England*. Available at www.history.ox.ac.uk

Bailey, M (2009) *The Agricultural History Review*. Volume 57 (1), pp25-31

Bailey, S.J (1948) The Countess Gundred's Lands. *The Cambridge Law Journal*. Volume 10(1) pp84-103. Cambridge University Press

Barefield, L (2002). Lineage and Women's Patronage: Mary of Woodstock and Nicholas Trevet's 'Les Cronicles'. *Medieval Feminist Forum 33*, pp21-30

Bartlett, W; Wright, T (1831). *The history and topography of the county of Essex, comprising its ancient and modern history*. Cambridge: Trinity College

Barlow, F (2013) *The Godwins: The Rise and Fall of a Noble Dynasty*. OXON: Routledge

Beltz, G.F (1871) *Memorials of the Order of the garter*. London: Pickering. p xlv

Bennett Connolly, S (2017) Heroines of the Medieval World. STROUD: Amberley

Bennett Connolly, S [online] www.historytheinterestingbits.com

Betham, William (1801). *The Baronetage of England*. LONDON: Miller

Bird, J (1922) ed. *The Augustinian Priory of St. John the Baptist, Holywell*, in Survey of London: Volume 8, Shoreditch. pp153-187. Available at British History Online

Bliss, W.H; Johnson, C (1897) ed. Regesta 180: 1347-1348, in *Calendar of Papal Registers Relating To Great Britain and Ireland: Volume 3, 1342-1362*, pp244-254, pp319-338. Available at British History Online

Blomefield, F (1806) 'Hundred of Earsham: Redenhall', in *An Essay Towards A Topographical History of the County of Norfolk*: Volume 5, pp358-372. Available at British History

Bloxham, M (1852). Sepulchral Monuments in Oxford Cathedral. *Royal Archaeological Institute (2013) The Archaeological Journal*. Volume 9, pp150-157. York: Archaeology Data Service. Available at https://doi.org/10.5284/1018054

Bolton, J.L (1985) *The Medieval English Economy 1150–1500*. LONDON: Dentcam

Bothwell, J (1997) Edward III and the 'New Nobility': Largesse and Limitation in Fourteenth Century England. *The English Historical Review*. Vol. 112(449) pp1111-1140. Oxford University Press

Bothwell, J (2004) *Edward III and the English Peerage: Royal Patronage, Social Mobility and Political Control in Fourteenth Century England*. Suffolk: Boydell Press

Bracton Online. Volume 2, pp250-1, available online at: amesfoundation.law.harvard.edu

Briggs, A (1984) *A Social History of England* LONDON: Book Club Associates

Burrow, J ed. (1974). *The History of the Norman Conquest of England by Edmund Freeman 1867 - 1879*. The University of Chicago Press

Butler, Sara (2001) Spousal Abuse in Fourteenth Century York: What can we learn from the Coroner's Rolls? *Florilegium* v18(2), pp61–78

Butler, Sara (2007) *The Language of Abuse: Marital Violence in Later Medieval England*. Lieden & Boston: Brill

Campbell, B.M.S (2010) Nature as historical protagonist: environment and society in pre-industrial England. *The Economic Historical Review* v63(2), pp281-314. Available at www.jstor.org

Carlton, R *No.24: Archaeological Fieldwork at Wark-on-Tweed, 2013 and 2015*. Available at www.flodden1513ecomuseum.org

Carter, A (1999). Dwale: An anaesthetic from Old England. *British Medical Journal* Volume 319(7225), pp1623–1626

Cassell's Illustrated History of England. Volume I (1865). London: Cassell Petter & Galpin Available on archive.org

Chandos Herald (1376–1387) *The Life & Feats of Arms of Edward the Black Prince* Translated and edited by Francisque-Michel (1883). London & Paris: Fotheringham. Available at archive.org.

Cockburn, J; King, H.P; McDonnell, K.G (1969) ed. Religious Houses: House of Carthusian monks, in *A History of the County of Middlesex: Volume 1, Physique, Archaeology, Domesday, Ecclesiastical Organization, the Jews, Religious Houses, Education of Working Classes To 1870, Private Education From Sixteenth Century*, pp159-169. Available at www.british-history.ac.uk

Cybulskie, D (2018) *Childhood in the Middle Ages*. Available at www.medievalists.net www.dhi.ac.uk, *Walter Espec, founder of Rievaulx abbey* (article)

Douche, R (1951) The Career, Lands and Family of William Montague, Earl of Salisbury,1301-44. *Bulletin of the Institute of Historical Research*. Volume 24(12) pp85–88

Dryburgh, P (2002) The Career of Roger Mortimer, first earl of March (c.1287-1330) Department of Historical Studies, March 2002

Fleming, P (2004). *Bristol Castle: A Political History*. The Bristol Branch of the Historical Association Local History Pamphlets.

Freeman, J; Stevenson, J (1987) 'Parishes: Fifield Bavant', in *A History of the County of Wiltshire:* Volume 13, South-West Wiltshire: Chalke and Dunworth Hundreds, ed. D A Crowley (London, 1987), pp60-66. Available at British History Online

Freeman, E (1873). *The History of the Norman Conquest of England, its causes and its results*. Volume 4. Oxford: Clarendon Press

Forster R, Yavari, N (2015) *Global Medieval: Mirrors for Princes Reconsidered*. Washington: Ilex Foundation and Harvard University Press

Gascony Rolls Project – Margaret Wake Source: GSR C61/52. Available from www. Gasconrolls.org

Gilchrist, R Olivia, M (1993) *Religious Women in Medieval East Anglia* Uni of East Anglia: Centre of East Anglian Studies 1.

Given-Wilson, C (2019). *Edward II 1307–1327*. London: Penguin Monarchs

Goodman, A (1968) Sir Thomas Hoo and the Parliament of 1376. Historical Research: *The Bulletin of the Institute of Historical Research*, vol. 41(104) pp139-149

Gransden, A (1972). The Alleged Rape by Edward III of the Countess of Salisbury in *The English Historical Review*. Volume 87(343) pp333-344. Oxford University Pres

Judith Green (1997) *Aristocracy of Norman England* pp378–379 Cambridge Uni Press

Green, M.A.E (1857) *Lives of the Princesses of England, from the Norman Conquest*. Volume 2. London: Longman

Hallam, E (1991) The Eleanor Crosses and Royal Burial Customs in *Eleanor of Castile 1290–1990. Essays to commemorate the 700th anniversary of her death* ed David Parsons. Stamford: Uni of Leicester

Hawkes, E (2002) Chapter 2, The 'Reasonable' Laws of Domestic Violence in Salisbury, E., Donavin, G., Price, L (2002) ed. *Domestic Violence in Medieval Texts*. Gainesville: University Press of Florida

Hefferan, M (2019) Edward III's household knights and the Crécy campaign of 1346 *Institute of Historical Research* Volume 92(255), pp24-29

Hicks, M (2016) *Two Tales of the Earls of Suffolk: Heirs Male and Heirs General*. Available at https://inquisitionspostmortem.ac.uk/

Hilton, Lisa (2008) *Queens Consort: England's Medieval Queens*. LONDON: Orion

Hollman, G (2019) *Royal Witches: From Joan of Navarre to Elizabeth Woodville*. Stroud: The History Press

Holmes, G (1957) *The Estates of the Higher Nobility in the Fourteenth Century*. Cambridge University Press

Horrox, R; Ormrod, M (2006) ed; *A Social History of England, 1200–1500*. Cambridge University Press

Jarvis, H, Rev (1886–1887) *Clare Priory*. The Suffolk Institute of Archaeology and Natural History, pp73-84. Ipswich: Pawsey and Hayes

Jessop, A (1908) The Coming of the Friars and other essays 5th ed. London. Unwin. Available at archive.org

Johnson, Ben (2021). *The Great Flood and Great Famine of 1314*. Available at https://www. historic-uk.com/ (article)

Jones, W.R (1970) The Court of the Verge: The Jurisdiction of the Steward and Marshal of the Household in Later Medieval England. *Journal of British Studies*. V10(1), pp1-29.

Jonker, M (2009) Estimation of life expectancy in the Middle Ages in *Journal of the Royal Statistical Society*. No.166, Part 1, pp105–117.

Jordan, W.C (2010). '*The Great Famine: 1315–1322 Revisited*,' in Scott Bruce, ed., Ecologies and Economies in Medieval and Early Modern Europe: Studies in Environmental History for Richard C. Hoffmann, pp45-62. Brill: Leiden.

Kerry, C. Rev (1892) Notes on the family of Strelley of Strelley, Oakerthorpe and Hazelbach *Derbyshire Archaeological Journal, Derbyshire Archaeological Society, 2016. (updated 2021)* Volume 14, pp72-118. Available at https://doi.org/10.5284/1038992

Kitzinger (2012). The 'window of opportunity' for death after severe brain injury: family experiences. In Sociology of Health & Illness. Volume 35(7), pp1095-1112

Knott, S. *Churches of East Anglia, Suffolk*. Available at www.suffolkchurches.co.uk

Lawne, P (2016) *The First Princess of Wales*. Stroud: Amberley Publishing

Lettenhove, K (1867-77. 25 volumes), Volume 3, *Oeuvres de Froissart, Chroniques*

Leyser, H. (1996) *Medieval Women: A Social History of Women in England 450–1500*. London: Phoenix Press

Mann, Ethel (1934) *Old Bungay* London: Heath Cranton

Margary, I.D (1973) 3rd ed. *Roman Roads in Britain*. London: John Baker

Marshall, A (2006a). The Childhood and Household of Edward II's Half-Brothers, Thomas of Brotherton and Edmund of Woodstock pp190-204. Dodd, G; Musson, A; ed. *In The Reign of Edward II*: New Perspectives. York Medieval Press

Marshall, A (2008) An Early Fourteenth-Century Affinity: The Earl of Norfolk and his Followers, pp1-12. Ed. Saul, N in *Fourteenth Century England Volume 5*. Suffolk: Boydell Press

Martin, E; Pendleton, C; Plouviez, J; Geake, H (2001) *Archaeology in Suffolk Proceedings*. Volume XL, part 2, pp201–236

McAleavy, T (1996) *Life in a Medieval Abbey*. English Heritage.

Mee, A (1941) *The King's England: Yorkshire West Riding* LONDON: Hodder and Stoughton. Available at archive.org

McKisack, M. (1959). *The Fourteenth Century 1307 -1399*. The Oxford University Press.

Mitchell, L (2011) Maud Marshal and Margaret Marshal: Two Viragos Extraordinaire, pp121-142. In *The Ties that Bind: Essays in Medieval British History in Honor of Barbara Hanawalt*. LONDON: Routledge

Mortimer, I (2006). *The Greatest Traitor: The Life of Sir Roger Mortimer, 1st Earl of March, Ruler of England, 1327-1330*. London: Pimlico

Mortimer, I (2008) *The Perfect King: The Life of Edward III, Father of the English Nation*. London: Vintage

Mortimer, I (2009) *The Time Travellers Guide to Medieval England*. London: Vintage

Mortimer, I Dr (2010). *Medieval Intrigue* LONDON: Continuum

Mortimer, I (2014) A note on the deaths of Edward II in *Notes and Essays*. Available at www.ianmortimer.com

Mortimer, R (1981). The Family of Rannulf de Glanville. *Bulletin of the Institute of Historical Research*. Volume LIV(129) pp1-16. University of London

Morris, M (2008). *A Great and Terrible King; Edward I and the Forging of Britain*. London: Hutchinson Random House

Mount, T (2014). *The Medieval Housewife and other women of the Middle Ages*. STROUD: Amberley

Musson, A ed, Powell, E (2009) *Crime, Law and Society in the Later Middle Ages*. Manchester University Press

Nalivaeva, N; Turner, A.J; Igor A. Zhuravin, I.A (2018). Role of Prenatal Hypoxia in Brain Development, Cognitive Functions, and Neurodegeneration Front *Neurosci*. Volume 12(825). Available at www.frontiersin.org

Nash, M.L (2019) *The History and Politics of Exhumation: Royal Bodies and Lesser Mortals.* London: Palgrave Macmillan

Nayling, N (1998) *The Magor Pill medieval wreck.* York: Council for British Archaeology

Northeast, P (2001) The Wills of the Archdeaconry 1439–1474; part 1. Suffolk Record Society: Boydell Press

Norton Bavant (1965) in *A History of the County of Wiltshire*: Volume 8, Warminster, Westbury and Whorwellsdown Hundreds, pp47-58. Available at British History Online

Olson, K (2020) Plague, famine and sudden death: 10 dangers of the medieval period. Available at www.historyextra.com

Orme, N. (2001). *Medieval Children.* New Haven : Yale University Press

Ormrod, M (2013) *Edward III.* Yale University Press

Packe, M (1983). *King Edward III* London: Routledge & Kegan Paul

Page, W (1906) ed. *Introduction to the Somerset Domesday, in A History of the County of Somerset*: Vol 1, pp383-432. Available at British History Online

Page W, Horace J (1907) Houses of Benedictine nuns: Abbey of Barking: *A History of the County of Essex:* Volume 2, pp115-122. Available at British History Online

Page, W (1911) ed. House of Cluniac monks: The priory of Montacute, *in A History of the County of Somerset*: Volume 2, pp111-115. Available at British History Online

Page, W (1975a) ed. Houses of Austin nuns: Priory of Campsey, in *A History of the County of Suffolk*: Volume 2, p112-115. Available at British History Online

Page, W (1975b) ed. House of Minoresses: Abbey of Bruisyard, in *A History of the County of Suffolk*: Volume 2, pp131-132. Available at British History

Panton, J.K (2011). *Historical Dictionary of the British Monarchy.* USA: Scarecrow Press

Platt, C. 1995. *The Abbeys and Priories of Medieval England.* London: Chancellor Press

PRME (2005) Edward III: November 1330 in *Parliament Rolls of Medieval England*, ed. Chris Given-Wilson, Paul Brand, Seymour Phillips, Mark Ormrod, Geoffrey Martin, Anne Curry and Rosemary Horrox. Available at British History Online [paid subscription]

Pobst, P (1996) ed. *The Register of William Bateman, Bishop of Norwich 1344–1355* vol 1. The Canterbury and York Society: Boydell Press.

Pobst, P (2000) ed. *The Register of William Bateman, Bishop of Norwich 1344–1355* vol 2. The Canterbury and York Society: Boydell Press

Podd, R (2020) Reconsidering maternal mortality in medieval England: aristocratic Englishwomen, c. 1236–1503 *Continuity and Change*. Volume 35, pp115–137. Available at doi:10.1017/S0268416020000156

Power, E (1922) *Medieval English Nunneries: 1275 to 1535.* Cambridge University Press

Prestwich, M (1997). *Edward I.* LONDON: Yale University Press

Prestwich, M (2005). *Plantagenet England 1225–1360.* OXFORD: Clarendon Press

Pugh, R.B; Crittal, E (1956) ed. Houses of Benedictine nuns: Abbey, later priory, of Amesbury In *A History of the County of Wiltshire:* Volume 3, pp242-259. Available at British History Online

Rees, W (1975) ed. *Calender of Ancient Petitions Relating to Wales.* University of Wales Press

Richardson, D (2002) *Another look at Margaret (Mowbray) Lucy.* https://soc.genealogy. medieval [article]

Richardson D (2007) *Hugh de Strauley (or Strelley), Esq., and his wife, Joyce Wykes.* Available at https://alt.talk.royalty.narkive.com/ [article]

Richardson, D (2008) *Kinsfolk of Sir Walter de Mauny, K.G.* Available at soc.genealogy. medieval (article)

Richardson, D (2011) 2nd ed. *Magna Carta Ancestry: A study in colonial and medieval families.* Volume 1

Richardson, D (2011) 2nd ed. *Plantagenet Ancestry: A Study in Colonial & Medieval Families,* New Greatly Expanded 2nd Edition, Vols. 1, 2 & 3

Ridgard J (1985) ed. *Medieval Framlingham Select Documents 1270–1524* Suffolk Records Society: Boydell Press

Robb, J., Cessford, C., Dittmar, J.M., Inskip, S., Mitchell, P.D. (2021) The greatest health problem of the Middle Ages? Estimating the burden of disease in Medieval England. *International Journal of Paleopathology.* Volume 34: pp101-112

Roskell, J.S; Clark, L; Rawcliffe, C (1993) ed. *The History of Parliament: the House of Commons 1386-1421.* Boydell and Brewer. [Sir Thomas Grey available at historyofparliamentonline.org]

Schofield, T. (2017). *Bungay Castle, Bungay, Suffolk; Geophysical Survey.* Needham Market: Suffolk Archaeology. https://doi.org/10.5284/1047366

Serjeantson, R.M; Adkins, W (1906) ed. *Houses of Austin canons: The priory of Chalcombe, in A History of the County of Northampton:* Volume 2, pp133-135. Available at www. british-history.ac.uk

Sharp, B. (2013). *Royal paternalism and the moral economy in the reign of Edward II: The response to the Great Famine.* The Economic day Review, 66(2), 628-647. Retrieved July 22, 2020, from www.jstor.org/stable/42921571

Staniland, K (1985). *Welcome, Royal Babe! The Birth of Thomas of Brotherton in 1300.* Costume Volume 19(1), pp1-13

Stapleton, T (1836) *A Brief Summary of the Wardrobe Accounts of the tenth, eleventh, and fourteenth years of King Edward the Second,* Archaeologia, Volume 26 (1836), p339

Stubbs, W (1861) *The Foundation of Waltham Abbey* OXFORD; LONDON: Parker

Suckling, A (1846) Bungay, in *The History and Antiquities of the County of Suffolk:* Volume 1, p119-161. Available at www.british-history.ac.uk

Suffolk Heritage Explorer *Building record BUN 006 - Church of St Mary and remains of Benedictine nunnery.* Available at http://heritage.suffolk.gov.uk

Suffolk Heritage Explorer *Monument record FML 001 - Framlingham Castle (Med).* Available at http://heritage.suffolk.gov.uk

Sumption J (2018) *Edward III 1327–1377.* Penguin Books

Swabey, F. (1999) *Medieval Gentlewoman: Life in a widow's household in the later middle ages.* Stroud: Sutton Publishing

TNA documents below available at https://discovery.nationalarchives.gov.uk/:

BCM/D/1/1/9 and 11
BCM/D/3
TNA BCM/D/5/101/8
TNA C/47/10/33/11
TNA E 101/394/19 (*Bruisyard inspectum 1356 from 1354*)
thehistoryjar.com, *Rules for Medieval Marriage* (article)
www.bl.uk, *The Ordinances of 1311.*

The Suffolk Institute of Archeaology and History Proceedings (1859), *On the Heraldry within the Abbey Gate at Bury St.Edmunds, as Evidence of its Date*: Vol 2, pp90-94 Available at https://suffolkinstitute.pdfsrv.co.uk

Tyson, B (1986). Jean le Bel: portrait of a chronicler. *Journal of Medieval History* Volume 12 (4), pp315–332

Verduyn, A (1995) The Selection and Appointment of Justices of the Peace in 1338 in *Historical Research*. Volume 68(165), pp1–25

Verity, B (2006). Love Matches and Contracted Misery: Thomas of Brotherton and his Daughters (Part 1). *Foundations of Medieval Genealogy* Volume 2(2), pp 91-111

Ward, J (1992) *English Noblewomen in the Later Middle Ages*. Essex: Longman

Ward, J (2002) *Women in Medieval Europe 1200–1500*. Essex: Pearson

Warner, K (2011b) *The Adherents of Edmund of Woodstock, Earl of Kent, in March 1330.* English Historical Review. Vol CXXVI (521). Oxford University Press.

Warner, K (2017a) Edward II. *The Unconventional King*. Stroud: Amberley

Warner, Kathryn (online) – see articles below at https://edwardthesecond.blogspot.com

Warner, K (2006) *The Feast of the Swan, 22 May 1306.*

Warner, K (2008a) *Sisters of Edward II (2): Joan of Acre*

Warner, K (2008b) *Edward II's Chamber Journal, 1322-1323*

Warner, K (2007a) *Birthday Wishes, Mortimer Ancestry, and Joan de Geneville*

Warner, K (2007b) *The Conspiracy of the Earl of Kent, 1330 (3)*

Warner, K (2010a) *The Children Of Richard Fitzalan, Earl Of Arundel*

Warner, K (2010b) *Marguerite Of France (1)*

Warner, K (2010c) *Marguerite of France (2)*

Warner, K (2011a) *William Montacute, Another Royal Favourite (1)*

Warner K (2012a) *Stay Away From The King, You Gascons (The Ordinaces)*

Warner, K (2012b) *19 October 1330: Edward III's Arrest Of Roger Mortimer*

Warner, K (2013a) *Edward II's Death And Afterlife Revisited (2)*

Warner, K (2013b) *Thomas of Brotherton's wedding, his daughter Margaret and his grandchildren*

Warner, K (2014a) *Edward II, Piers Gaveston and Isabella's Jewels That Weren't*

Warner, K (2014b). *The Children of Edmund of Woodstock and Margaret Wake, and Joan of Kent's Date of Birth*

Warner, K (2015) *Marriage Negotiations between England and Aragon in Edward II's Reign*

Warner, K (2016) *The Date of Birth and Siblings of Philippa of Hainault, Queen of England*

Warner K (2017b) *Thomas, Lord Wake (1298-1349)*

Warner, K (2019) *The Life and Tragic Death of Alice of Norfolk*

Warner, K (2020) *Jousting 1323*

Warner, K (2022) *Margaret of Norfolk*

Wark Castle. See www.castlesfortsbattles.co.uk and www.northofthetyne.co.uk

Water, R.E.C (1878) *Genealogical memoirs of the extinct family of Chester. Volume 1*, pp328-330. London: Robson & Sons

Weever, J (1767) *Antient funeral monuments*. London. Available at archive.org

Weir, A (2008) *Britain's Royal Families; The Complete Genealogy*. London: Vintage Press

Wentersdorf, K (1979). The clandestine marriages of the fair maid of Kent. *Journal of Medieval History*. Volume 5, pp203-231

White, W (1844) White's Gazetteer and Directory of Suffolk, p428. Sheffield: Leader

Wilson-Lee K (2019) *Daughters of Chivalry: The Forgotten Children of Edward I* LONDON: Picador

Wrottesley, G (1898) *Crecy and Calais*. LONDON: HMO. Available at archive.org

Wrottesley, G (1905) *Pedigrees from the Plea Rolls*. Available at archive.org

Wyatt, L. (2018) *Secret Chepstow*. Stroud: Amberley

Wyatt, L (2019a) *Secret Monmouth*. Stroud: Amberley

Wyatt, L. (2019b) *A History of Nursing*. Stroud: Amberley

Index